Shadows Chant

AEONA'S HEART

Paul Outram

WOHLER PUBLISHING

First published in the United Arab Emirates in 2025 by Wohler Publishing

and imprint Wohler Publishers.

This edition published in 2025

Text copyright: WOHLER 2024

The moral rights of the author have been asserted.

ISBN: 978-1-068462016

Disclaimer

This story and its characters are entirely fictitious. Unless otherwise indicated, all names, characters, businesses, places, events, and incidents in this book are either the product of the author's imagination or used fictitiously. Any resemblance to actual persons, living or dead, or actual events is purely coincidental. The author strongly recommends consulting medical professionals for any injury, whether minor or severe. The events, actions, and dialogues within this book are intended for self-help and fictional purposes only.

All rights reserved

No part of this publication may be reproduced, stored in retrieval system, or transmitted, in any form or by any means, without the prior permission in writing from the publisher, nor otherwise circulated in any form of binding or cover other than that in which it if published and without a similar condition including this condition being imposed on the subsequent purchaser.

Dedication

A very special thanks to Megan D'Costa

for her valuable contribution and editing.

Printed and bound in U.A.E by Wohler Publishers

The paper and board used in this book are made from wood from responsible sources

WOHLER PUBLISHING

www.shadowschant.com

You Are Not Alone

The primary focus of this book is to support your mental, physical, and emotional wellbeing, not forgetting your self-worth. Aeona went through many sorrowful things throughout her journey. It was very difficult for her, but like her, you will move forward in life and grow.

There are so many things that are thrown at us in life, whether it is the loss of a loved one, loneliness when people move away, or being pushed away. Not to mention our struggles at school or with the many negative people around us, which can cause us to forget to love ourselves.

This book is dedicated to you, because you deserve to be loved.

Aeona will be our emotional support as she talks you through her ups and downs in this book. She will reflect on her emotional journey and discuss some of the things that helped mend her broken heart.

FORWARD

'AEONA'S HEART'

This supplemental guide to Shadows Chant invites readers into a profound exploration of grief, guilt, forgiveness, and healing, all from the perspective of a teenager. I know that some of the topics discussed may bring back memories of the event. It may be painful or sensitive, but to heal, you need to let yourself breathe and come to terms with the past, thereby releasing yourself from the burden.

Writing about a child who accidentally causes the death of close family members, especially when it is a twin and her father, was heart-breaking at times. I wanted to create a world filled with emotion that readers could reflect on and connect with. Through Aeona's emotional journey, she encountered things beyond her control, and you were able to experience her sadness and loneliness, and witness some of her healing.

In creating the characters for the story, I initially wrote Christopher as the main character, but incorporating a sibling at the beginning allowed me to introduce several different emotional factors for the reader to consider deeply. I must admit, there were times when I felt emotional about what I was putting the poor girl through. This book does not shy away from the painful truths that many teenagers have to endure on a daily basis, even if they do not want to admit it.

I hope this book offers you guidance and reminds you, that you are never truly alone.

We all need someone to listen,

not just when we're smiling,

but when we are struggling through the day.

Letter from Aeona to You

Hi there,

First... thank you for reading my letter. I know we have a lot to talk about.

If you are lonely, feeling guilty about something you have done, have other things on your mind, or are feeling sad, I want you to know something really important: it is not your fault, it is never your fault, and I am with you, walking hand in hand, side by side. You are never alone.

We have been through a lot, you and I. Some days are really hard. But I promise you, they do get easier, bit by bit. You are allowed to cry. You are allowed to miss people. You are allowed to laugh again.

We will get through our pain. We are going to talk about all of the things on our minds and take our time in doing so.

We are stronger than we think.

With love

Aeona ♡

Contents

You Are Not Alone 5

FORWARD 6

A Letter from Aeona to You 8

1. Loss, Bereavement, and Grief 11
2. Feeling Lonely? 30
3. It's Okay to Talk 38
4. When Someone Blames You 47
5. Big Feelings Are Normal 56
6. Taking Responsibility 59
7. Making Amends 62
8. Understanding Addiction 65
9. When to Get Professional Help 81
10. Crushing Hard 84
11. Infatuation vs. Unconditional Love 99
12. Hate in the Mirror 108
13. Understanding Food 121
14. Binge and Purge 126
15. Anorexia - a suffering disappearance 134
16. Understanding Self-Harm 142
17. Self-Help 148
18. When to Get Professional Help 154
19. Self-Destruction 156

20. Parents.. 166

21. When love hurts!... 178

22. Why Do They Blame Me?.................................... 182

23. Gradual distancing... 187

24. Dealing with Sibling Favouritism........................ 192

25. What If I'm Afraid to Tell?.................................. 196

26. Divorce or Separation.. 205

27. Between Two Worlds 215

28. Impermanence 224

29. Compassion and Self-Forgiveness 230

30. Self Forgiveness 241

31. Introduction to Happiness................................... 250

32. Discovering Your Purpose................................... 266

TELEPHONE HELPLINES 273

EUROPE... 275

AMERICAS & THE CARIBBEAN 281

MIDDLE EAST & NORTH AFRICA 286

AFRICA 289

ASIA & PACIFIC 297

1. Loss, Bereavement, and Grief

Aeona started life in a loving family; some children don't have that, but for her, it was a reality. She had her twin brother, Christopher, and the two of them were always playing, laughing, and sometimes even arguing, just like siblings do. Their dad, Thomas, always kissed them goodbye every morning before work and turned everything into a game, while their mum, Anwen, was the serious one who made sure they cleaned their room and focused on their schoolwork. You may come from something different from this. You might live with your mum, your dad, or in another home, but one thing is for sure: remember that you're loved.

At the beginning of *Shadows Chant*, Aeona and Christopher started a new year at school. They were excited but also a little nervous; moving from primary to secondary school is a big step. At the same time, Aeona was getting closer to finally having her own room. She felt like her life was just beginning.

But then, one night, everything changed.

A terrible accident destroyed their home, and with it... Aeona lost her brother, her father, and Jinx, her pet cat. She survived, but it felt like her whole world had turned to ash.

When someone we love, or have a connection with, dies, we feel something called grief.

Is grief different from sadness?

In short, yes. It's similar to sadness, but it's a much deeper and more complex feeling.

Sadness is an emotion we feel when we're disappointed. Grief, on the other hand, is a complex and ongoing process that happens when a person or pet passes away, is no longer with you, or has gone to another place. It's an emotional response to a significant loss, often involving waves of sadness, but also anger, guilt, confusion, numbness, and even relief or peace at times. It can affect not just your feelings, but also your thoughts, body, and behaviour. So, while sadness is part of grief, grief is more than just feeling sad.

Aeona went through this when she looked for her brother in the hospital. She was unaware that he was gone. It wasn't until her mother told her the horrible news and to add to it, that her father was gone too that she understood. She'd lost the people she loved.

When someone dies and you miss them so much that it hurts, it can be very overwhelming at times. This feeling can happen at any time and may last for a while. When you keep remembering your loved one, it can feel just as painful as when they first died.

Blame is another thing that might go through a person's mind when someone dies. When Aeona thought about her family members, she blamed herself for going to the kitchen. She regretted wanting a drink of water. The 'what if' questions went around and around in her head. There are many different emotions discussed in this book, and you should always read the later chapters, 'Compassion & Self-Forgiveness' and 'Happiness', when things feel really upsetting.

Aeona blamed herself for what happened to her

family. This is why we're going to reflect on her emotional wellbeing, in the hope that she'll help you understand that we all need to be kind to ourselves. She had to deal with a great deal of emotional trauma. Grief and regret sometimes go hand in hand. If you've lost someone, you might have heard words like passed or went away. You might have been told, 'They aren't with us anymore; they've gone to heaven' (depending on your belief).

When a person you loved is no longer here, you can still remember them and cherish the love you shared.

Sometimes you might feel:

Angry at the world or the people around you
Like you don't want to talk or do anything

Tired, or maybe you can't sleep
Like you want to cry, but the tears won't come
Or you cry all the time and don't know how to stop

Aeona felt many of these things, but she will get through it… I assure you, and so will you. I know it might not feel like it at times. When she was in the hospital, she had plenty of time to reflect on what had happened. Some days she stayed in bed. Some days she wanted to scream, but slowly, she found small things that helped.

When we discuss Aeona and her emotions at various points in the story, we can see what helped and what didn't. I'm not saying everything will work for you, because we're all different and special in our own unique way, and we all process hurt differently. Some things may seem too difficult, or you may not be emotionally ready for them right now. It's okay to feel like this! You can take things as slowly or as quickly as you feel comfortable. There's no set timeframe for picking yourself up. This slow process is about a very special person… and that's you. Take as much time as you need.

No one has to go through grief alone. No one should go through anything alone, not you, not anyone. When I say you'll find someone who listens and cares, I mean it. They may be the next person you meet today or tomorrow, but I hope that people you trust

gather around to listen, guide, and love you.

Memory Journal

Aeona wrote about her brother's jokes and her dad's bedtime stories. It made her cry, but it also made her feel close to them.

When Aeona was at the library, she was searching for information about the Lambton Worm. She first saw a picture of it, which made her laugh. An image jumped into her mind of when she and Christopher both had chickenpox and had spots all over their faces. She used to call him her little Dalmatian. As she drew the picture, she smiled, thinking about him. She also put a smiley face at the bottom of the paper to remind her of him. I kept some of these subtle details hidden from readers… I felt they were Aeona's personal thoughts, and part of her healing and wellbeing. She also created a 'Memory Journal' to preserve the sparkle of happiness she shared with her loved ones. Her memories… your memories, are still there, deep in your heart, and never forgotten.

Mary and the counsellors, Samira and Naomi, helped her start a Memory Journal. There were times when she had recurring nightmares that she couldn't shake. She would sometimes creep into Nyxa's room, where she'd be distracted by talking about Christopher and her father.

'Tell me about your brother, Aeo?'

'What did he like to play with?'

'What did your father look like?'

It was all to push the dark thoughts away. Nyxa also wrote in a journal and told Aeona about the good times she had with her mother, but what happened to her was a little different. We'll discuss 'regret' later in the book. You can see that they both wrote in journals to help them remember their loved ones. Nyxa felt heartbreak, which is a little different from grief, as her mother hadn't died; after the accident, she just couldn't care for her daughter.

Find happiness in your memories. Sometimes you may think you're forgetting them, but that doesn't mean you will. They'll always be with you and pop into your head when you least expect them. Writing everything down is a lovely way to remember them. Please don't let the journal make you feel sad. Every letter, every word, every full stop shows that you love them.

Talk to Someone

It was difficult for Aeona at first, as she felt she had no one. Nurse Gina, who looked after her in the hospital, tried to speak to her about losing her loved ones, but at that time, it was just too soon. However, the sooner you talk to someone about your feelings, the better. Holding onto things can make it worse in the long run, but take all the time you need, my friend.

It can be very tough if you haven't got anyone to talk to or trust. But, for the time being, don't be embarrassed if you'd like to talk to the person who's died. It's quite normal and healthy to do this. Aeona still talks to Christopher sometimes: she tells him when she's scared or when something funny happens. He gave her so much to hold onto when he was alive. She wrote him little notes and letters from time to time. She also remembers her dad's silly bedtime stories and how he used to throw her over his shoulder and swing her around like a superhero. These memories still make her sad, but they also make her smile. Think about what they used to like; maybe you could download their favourite song, or one you remember listening to with them. Perhaps you could light a candle for them, like Aeona does on their birthday. These little things help her feel connected to their memory.

Having friends who listen to you is a good thing, and hopefully, you can talk to them. However, I understand that sometimes, it's not that easy. You might feel that they'll judge you or that you feel they'll think you're weak, and should just move on with life. Understand that everyone is different and we all handle things in different ways. The way you're dealing with it is just your way! No right or wrong, just your way. Simple and straightforward, it's how you're trying to cope. If you're unsure about approaching someone, try gauging the question before opening up. Why not start with, 'Can I ask you something? Have you lost anyone close to you?' If they brush it off as if it's nothing, you might want to try someone else, but don't give up; you'll be surprised by how many people are going through the same thing. Although it may feel incredibly hard, you will pull through; just give it time. The big question is, 'But how long?' Well, that's a tough one. The truth is, no one knows. A day, a week, a month… take all the time you need.

We know Aeona couldn't talk to her mum, but you need to understand adults can also have issues dealing with the death of a family member. I have no excuse for the way Anwen treated her daughter, but I wanted to highlight that adults and parents can have issues of dealing with loss and grief. She needed specialist help straight away. The sad thing is she didn't reach out to anyone. Like I said, everyone is different. Aeona needed her, but at that time, her mother couldn't cope and so vented her grief through anger, blaming her daughter.

Talking to a counsellor may be an option you could try. Hopefully, they're approachable, someone who'll listen to what you're going through, not only with the loss of a person you loved, but with everything else in this guide. Counsellors are trained to help children and teenagers open up and discuss ways of coping with and navigating difficult times. If you feel that you don't trust them or that they'll just call your parents, try someone else. How about a female teacher? I am referring to females, as they have generally been hardwired with the skills of parenthood. However, this does seem a little ironic for poor Aeona, but this is why I use the word 'generally'. If you're a boy, having a discussion with a male teacher might work for you. A point to note: teachers must report serious issues, as it concerns your safeguarding. Grief isn't one of them, unless you feel it's becoming too much. Please talk to someone about how you're feeling.

Breathing Breaks

To help calm herself down or when she felt like she was going to have a panic attack, Aeona did some breathing exercises. Whenever she had a memory of Christopher or her father, she would try very, very hard to sit still, taking deep breaths through her nose and blowing out through her mouth. These attacks happened a lot in the hospital, and sometimes when she was alone. When she was at the Cross Fell hut in chapter twenty-two, she woke up in a panic, nearly waking the man. A nightmare can trigger a panic attack. It's okay to have the occasional nightmare; you have no control over them, but identifying triggers is a good start to lessen how often they occur.

Aeona would sit quietly, breathing in through her nose and out through her mouth. Counting slowly... one-in one-out, two-in two-out, three-in three-out, four-in four-out, five-in five-out. It worked most of the time; sometimes, it would take longer for her heart rate to settle and the dark images to fade. Eventually, she would lie back down, picture herself kissing Christopher on his cheek, before drifting off back to sleep.

Breathing through the nose helps to calm you down.

Scientists say that we have a nerve at the back of our nose, which is like a 'relaxing nerve.' It reduces the 'fight or flight' response in our bodies and improves our lung function, lowers our heart rate, and lowers our blood pressure.

Could you please give it a try for me? I want you to feel relaxed. Nothing more, nothing less... close your eyes and focus on feeling the air moving in and out. You can do this anytime and anywhere you're feeling anxious about something. Not just when a memory triggers something unpleasant, but also for exams, dealing with hurtful people, or overcoming a phobia.

Nature Calms

Aeona spent most of her time outside, whether in the sky on the back of dragon or on the ground, thinking about her next move. I understand that you haven't got a mythical creature comforting, listening, and supporting you.

Think about your own wellbeing! You're aware of the little things that can be upsetting. If you try to remember what you were doing before you felt sad or angry, you can try to avoid these things. We call these triggers. There may be something outside that upsets you or makes you cry. It's okay to feel this way. It is the same for any of these possible ways of helping you feel better. If even one of my tips helps you for even a moment, my heart is truly happy for you.

Going outside, you may see trees, grass, the desert, and possibly feel the wind on your face. Depending on where you live or what climate you're in, being outside can help you relax. Think about Aeona; at times, she felt a strong sense of grief, and many triggers brought traumatic memories flooding back. For her, they revolved around being in a house; this is why she liked the outdoors. Generally, everything about them was a trigger for her loss, her memories, her sadness. Emotional triggers stemming from a landing, a kitchen, or a cooker. Sometimes these can be as small as a creaky step or even a particular sound. Outside, Aeona felt free, the wind a constant calm in her eyes. It distracted her from her grief. However, remember that it can come and go at any time. If it does, try to focus on the good memories, don't let the sadness push you down. Smile at the cherished moments you had. It's not a time for pain; try to turn the event into love. The love you shared, the happiness you should relive, the love you will carry forward.

Safe Space Box

Aeona also created a Safe Space Box, a special place to store her treasured belongings.

Mary introduced Aeona to the idea and taught her how it had helped her. You might think, 'Why would an adult want a Safe Space Box?' They can feel hurt too, from losing someone they care about. Mary's memories weren't in a box exactly. They were in her special place in the dining room. Do you remember the knitted doll in the cabinet? Adults go through the same feelings as you, and it helps them keep their memories alive.

Let's read through Aeona's experience in Shadows Chant again.

'Along the side of the dining room, an old wooden cabinet stood, its shelves cluttered with ornaments: a delicate lady in a flowing purple gown, captured mid-dance, her porcelain feet barely touching the ground, her arms stretched upward, frozen in graceful movement as though caught in the swirl of music. Beside her, a knitted doll with uneven stitches sat propped up against the glass, its button eyes a little too large for its round face, the yarn hair messy and tangled, its small arms outstretched as if reaching for a hug.'

All of these were given to her by her husband, Ronald, and they deserved a place in her cabinet. Each subtle detail reflected the love they shared. Whether it was a place, a time, or an event they shared. Good memories, objects, notes, and drawings are like souvenirs of love.

Aeona's box didn't contain much, as most of her father and brother's things were lost in the fire, but she did have a couple of things that had been kept in the garage, such as one of her father's caps, a drawing her brother had done, and a little funny-haired troll he had given her. Whenever she missed them, she would take the box out from under her bed. The memories would smile back at her, wanting to be touched, read, and played with. The feel of them in her hands would bring back the beautiful memories they shared.

Expressing your emotions

You could write a letter or a grief diary to the person you miss. Why not tell them what you've been doing? You could also remind them of things you did together.

'I went to the park today. It was different without you. Do you remember when we would run up and down the slide? It was so much fun. Oh, and that time I fell off the swing.'

Say whatever you want; they'll always be part of your heart. You can't just switch from one emotion to the other and expect everything to be okay. We both know it's not as easy as that. And this is why, together, we are going to look at some of the things you can do to help you cope with losing a loved one.

I don't know if you enjoy drawing or doodling, but

you can express your feelings through angry scribbles, quiet shapes, or anything you like. Doing angry scribbles doesn't mean you have 'anger issues' and DON'T let anyone say so! Being angry is a normal emotion. We all get angry at some things, and getting angry because you lost a loved one is no different. So many questions could be going through your head, like: 'What if I…?' or 'Why didn't I…?' Don't think about these at the moment. These have more to do with 'regret' than grief. We can discuss the differences

between them later.

Releasing or letting go of your emotions is better than bottling them up. I know you may feel vulnerable talking about what's in your heart, but Aeona had dragon, who listened. People sometimes don't know how to just, listen. They think they need to fix you… like you're broken. Yes, it sounds silly, but it's their way of showing they love you, in their own way.

When you feel like screaming! Either let it out into a pillow or get some paper and some crayons. If you choose the latter or both, you still get the paper.

Choose a colour that reflects the way you feel.

Yellow, orange, dark blue, green, red, dark blue, purple, grey, black.

Then, close your eyes and see the emotion as a physical thing in your mind. Feel the crayon in your hand, feel its hardness as it touches the page. Press as hard as the emotion, feel it coming out in sharp, zig-zags, slashes, hard lines, sharp shapes, anything that you feel building inside.

Another way to do it is to have a 'Safe-Anger Zone,' instead of letting the anger and grief out freely, as if it is in control of you. Draw a box and scribble your anger inside, storms, dark clouds. Let it have control of you, the silent scream on the page. As you vent your emotions, count down: ten, nine, eight, seven, six, five, four, three, two, one. Then throw the crayon across the room. It doesn't deserve to be near you. Next, pick the first calm colour you see, pastel colours: light blue, mauve, beige, lilac, pink. Try to think about a beautiful thing you shared with your loved one. You can draw something meaningful or create slow, calming lines. The crayon feels different now... it wants to be in your hand, soft, gentle, and loved. Press gently, breathing slowly in through your nose and out through your mouth. Don't focus on the inside of the box.

You have a beautiful heart and mind, and deserve to love yourself and let go.

Some days are better than others. It's okay to have fun. Smiling doesn't mean you've forgotten them. It's

okay to be sad, too. Crying helps to let out the pain you have. You are not the only one going through this.

Your feelings are valid.

Everyone needs help... everyone, no matter how old or young you are. You might not want to reach out. I know, it's hard to reach out and find someone who listens. Bottling your emotions up is only a short-term fix. You can feel the pressure in your chest, like you are holding your breath, they niggle at your mind. You can push them down, but to heal properly, you need to release the pain, talking, scribbling, screaming into a pillow, but please do something.

Aeona tried to bottle it up by distracting herself with other things. But she let it get the better of her a couple of times. Remember, when she went to school in chapter fifteen: 'doing art, and a boy near her was drawing dinosaurs, monsters, or something, and then, she just picked up her chair and started smashing it on his table, hitting the boy in the process. She then ran to the corner of the class, hid in the cupboard, and pulled the door behind her. It took the deputy head more than thirty minutes to get her out, and then she said, "Aeona became extremely violent."

It takes courage to talk, I hear you. Some people you can trust, some you can't. Some people will listen without judgement. Some people won't. It's like a little game… ask the right questions and you'll find out who's a good listener. I truly hope you can find

someone you can trust with your deepest emotions.

When to Ask for Help?

Aeona had days when she just couldn't deal with the grief by herself. In truth, I placed people in her way, ones she would come to trust. I hope you find people who can help, not that you have to trust them right away, but I do hope you find someone who will listen.

Please seek help if:

- You feel like nothing matters.

- You can't sleep or eat properly

- You think about hurting yourself.

Asking for help is a sign of strength, not weakness. I hope you have a loving family with whom you can talk. If you feel like you don't want to or can't talk to them about your loss, understand that grown-ups like teachers or counsellors can help or at least listen.

You can also call or message support services if you ever need someone right away. There are people trained to talk to young people, like yourself, who are going through tough times.

At the back of this book, you will find a lot of help lines and websites you can call. If you are a little nervous about giving them your name, you don't have to. Call anonymously and then, when you have built some trust with the person on the line, please let them help you.

You are brave.
You are loved.
You are never alone.

2. Feeling Lonely?

What Is Loneliness?

First of all, we need to understand that loneliness is a little different from being alone. We can feel lonely even when we're sitting in a classroom, or when we have all of our family around us. It's a strange feeling, like an ache inside us when something is missing. It can feel like a part of our world has gone quiet, like a toy that's been lost and can't be replaced. This is loneliness.

I'm truly sorry if you're feeling this way. After grief can come loneliness, but it doesn't just come from someone passing away. A terrible emptiness in your heart can stir up many feelings, like sadness, anger, confusion, and even fear. It can be hard to describe what you're feeling, as there are many different emotions that swim around together as one emptiness.

There are so many reasons for feeling lonely. You were by Aeona's side through her tough times, when she was lonely. It might have been better if she'd known you were reading about her; then she might have felt differently. Perhaps a family member used to pick you up from school, and now no one waits for you at the gate. Or maybe your best friend or pet has passed away, and now your house feels quieter and emptier. You might miss hearing their voice, feeling their hugs, or laughing at their jokes. But sometimes a person you liked suddenly stops talking to you, the group you were in decides that you don't belong, or someone moves to another place. The list goes on and on. Even if you try to have fun, it just doesn't feel the same. Sometimes, it can feel like no one really understands what you're going through, but believe me, they do.

Aeona was in the ICU when she first felt the hollow ache of emptiness settle in her heart. She was utterly alone. The grief of losing Thomas and Christopher overwhelmed her. She also lost her beloved cat, Jinx. Later on, she lost Fluff, her hamster, and then Nyxa. She went through a lot of bad things: grief, rejection, and loneliness. When one or two negative emotions mount up, it can deepen the isolation a person feels. (See the chapters 'Parents' and 'Why Do They Blame Me?')

You might feel the darkness around you, a sense of isolated loneliness, but you'll find glimmers of hope. Aeona saw hope while staying with Mary, and she discovered the light in Nyxa. Eventually, she was able to find real comfort in dragon. Her story isn't over, and neither is yours.

Loneliness can manifest in various ways. Sometimes it makes your chest feel heavy. Other times, it might make you want to cry or stay in your room. Perhaps you'd like to be quiet and not talk to anyone. Or maybe you get angry more easily and don't know why. All of these reactions are normal. Your heart is just trying to adjust to a big change. When someone moves or you don't have anyone to talk to, it can leave you with a vast emptiness in your heart. It's essential to know that you're not alone in feeling this way. Many other young people and adults also feel lonely. Even if they don't talk about it, these feelings are common. You aren't strange, bad, or wrong for feeling lonely. You're a wonderful person. And being you means you love those around you, and we all hurt deeply when we get left behind or pushed aside.

Think of loneliness like this: imagine your heart is a cosy room. When the person you loved was with or near you, it was like they held a special light in that room, and now that they're gone, it feels like someone's turned it off.

*The room isn't broken,
but it feels darker.*

You might bump into things or feel unsure of what to do next, like a cold distraction affecting your focus. But even though it feels dark right now, that light can and will come back. It might not look exactly the same as before, but a new light, a new warmth, can grow over time. Aeona was able to connect with different people who came into her life, and as her story unfolds, more people will come into her life, and yours… believe me, they will.

Sometimes you, Aeona included, worry that if you talk about how lonely you feel, you'll make other people sad or upset. However, the truth is that talking about your loneliness can help it feel smaller. You don't have to pretend to be okay if you're not. It's brave to say, "I miss them," or "I feel alone." Sharing your feelings with someone you trust, such as a parent, teacher, grandparent, or friend, can make a significant difference. Just saying your feelings out loud, to yourself or writing them in a notebook, can help your heart feel a little lighter.

It's also okay if you don't always want to talk. Some people the same age as you draw pictures of how they feel. Others play with small things, such as toys, or go outside and move around to help themselves feel better. Please, don't throw yourself into your phone. Just think, if Aeona had her phone, she would have acted quite differently throughout the story.

She didn't have it in the hospital, obviously due to the terrible accident. She never had her phone when she was staying with Mary. If she'd had her phone, do you think she would have gone into the living room and sat watching Nyxa? The simple answer is no, she wouldn't have. She yearned for someone her own age to talk to. Just think for a second: imagine if Aeona and Nyxa had been engrossed in their screens. Do you think they would have bonded? Spoken to each other? Listened to each other's hearts? Or had someone who cared or listened without judgement? Nyxa had a phone, but she distracted herself with her books. She was also very, very lonely. She never felt close to the other children who came through the Home. It wasn't really until Aeona appeared that she was able to break down some of her walls and open up to her kindred spirit, a girl who'd been through so much hardship, like herself.

You're a beautiful person who knows that although phones are great things to hide away in, they can also increase your loneliness. The two girls needed each other for comfort and support. Think about this for a moment. Would the phone have helped them? The answer is yes and no. The phone is a quick fix, but at the end of the day, if you don't reach out to anyone, literally anyone, it will only reflect your face on the cold, black screen with no one to share comfort with.

There's no one 'right way' of dealing with loneliness. What matters the most is knowing that it's real, it's okay to have it, but it won't last forever. It might come and go. Some days you'll feel okay, and then other days, like birthdays, holidays, or quiet rainy or hot days, it might come back stronger. This is normal. Your heart is learning how to cope with the isolation of someone who isn't physically there anymore. It might feel unfair; you might have done something that the others didn't like. I'm not saying you did, but these things happen from time to time in relationships. A group of friends can shift in one direction, change, or follow other interests as you move through life. You need to care about yourself, and you'll find your path and find other friends.

It's a big job getting out of loneliness, and it's okay; take your time, it will pass. Remember: even though it might feel like you're the only one in the world that feels this way, you aren't alone.

When Aeona was flying high in the air upon the dragon's back, the rushing wind in her ears, the patchwork fields below, but the silence of it all was lonely. Pure, dark loneliness ate at her heart. Her dad waving through the car's windscreen, blowing kisses as he went off to work, and being carried upstairs like she was a superhero. Not forgetting the final words of her brother, "Where are you going?" echoed in her ears. The "Shhh! You'll wake Mum and Dad" of her own voice whispered in the wind, back at her. These all brought the feeling rushing back at her. Loneliness can come back when you least expect it. This is what memories can do, depending on when they come flooding back.

You may not see them, yet, but there are people around you who care. Like Aeona, be strong my friend. And, even though it doesn't feel like it, your heart is stronger than you think.

Why do we feel lonely?

When someone alienates you or something happens, it can make you feel utterly alone; it can feel like a piece of your world has just disappeared. You might be used to talking to that person, playing with them, hugging them, or just knowing they were around. Now they're not, which can make your heart hurt. It's like having your favourite book taken away before you finish reading it. You can still read other books, but it's not the same, and you miss what you had. That missing feeling in your heart, that empty space, is where loneliness often begins.

One helpful thing to do is to notice how you're feeling and try to name it. You can say to yourself, "Right now I feel like being alone," or "I feel mad and I don't know why," or "I miss them so much today."

Naming your feelings helps you understand them.

It also helps the people around you understand how to support you. If you don't want to say it out loud, you can write it down in a notebook or draw a picture. Some young people like using colours to express how they feel, such as blue for sadness, red for anger, or grey for loneliness.

No matter how you feel, you are allowed to feel it. Your way of grieving is your own, and it matters. You don't have to be like anyone else. You just have to be honest with yourself and kind to your heart.

3. It's Okay to Talk

One of the best ways to help with loneliness is to talk about it. Talking helps us feel less alone, even if it's just a little bit. It's like shining a flashlight in a dark room; it doesn't make the room full of sunshine, but it helps you see what's around. Think about how dragon and Aeona talked about her father and brother. It was a way for her to open up and talk about the cherished memories she had of them.

Aeona wanted to tell Christopher so much about the dragon. She knew he would have gone crazy just to see it. Funny, she told dragon, she thought her father would have been scared of it at first, but would have let her keep it anyway. This made her smile a lot. Dragon was a little wary when Aeona talked about them, but glad she did because it knew how much she cared for them. It liked hearing the stories of her father, camping, playing in the garden, and missing him dearly every time he had to go to work in the morning. And then she would have a little 'lonely' time where she would be very quiet. It was okay for her to be silent, lost in thought. After ten minutes or so, sometimes more, dragon would quietly distract her to bring her out of the gloom. There were times it was worried about mentioning her mother, as it didn't want to bring back the hurtful memories.

The important part is letting your feelings out in some way. Keeping everything inside can make you feel lonelier. I know it sounds a little cliché, but burying or building a wall around your heart and yourself is a sure-fire way not to let go. Aeona bottled up her emotions and as you see, it sent her down a very dark hole. It was very sad for her, but at that time, she never had anyone to talk to. Nyxa came and went, but everything changed once she found someone to really talk to. Yes, I know it was a dragon, but with patience, a special friend will come into your life when you least expect it. Until they come along, if you feel that no one is listening, pretend your toy is dragon. It doesn't matter what you do, but please just talk.

One night in her bedroom, Aeona wrote a letter to her dad. She told him everything she wished she could say to him. She didn't send it anywhere, but writing it made her feel a little closer to him, and a little less lonely. Imagine carrying a rucksack or backpack full of big rocks. Every time you talk about your feelings, it's like taking one rock out. The backpack might still be there, but it gets lighter each time. That's what talking does: it helps you breathe easier. Or like a very tight balloon pushing out your chest, every time you talk, a tiny bit of air is released, and eventually you will be able to breathe gently in through your nose, and finally have the control you need.

Sometimes you might not want to talk because you're worried you'll cry. And that's okay, too. Crying is nothing to be ashamed of. Grown-ups cry, and even animals feel sad sometimes. It is just another way your heart speaks when words are too hard to say. So, if you cry while talking, that's okay. It's normal. It's brave. That sounds silly doesn't it - Brave crying? It takes a lot to let your emotions out, even just a little… so yes… it is brave.

Have a read through the following, which may also help you when you're feeling lonely.

Write or draw how you feel.

Put the paper or notebook in your special place.

'I really miss _____ because we used to __.'

'One thing I wish I could say to them is _____.'

'Sometimes I feel lonely when _____.'

'When I feel sad, it helps me to _____.'

'One memory that makes me smile is _____.'

You can also use these as a way to start a conversation with someone you trust, or write, or draw how you feel. By doing this, you may be able to see a pattern in your ups and downs.

How do I Feel Today?

Draw an emoji for each time you feel down, but please remember the happy times, too.

☺ Happy   😢 Sad   😕 Confused   ☹ Lonely

😠 Angry   😐 Okay   💤 Tired   ♥ Loved

Why do you think you feel this way?

_____

A Good Memory I Want to Keep

Think of a happy memory with the person. Write about or draw a picture of it.

This memory makes me feel: (circle)

☺ Happy   😢 Sad   ♥ Loved   ✦ Peaceful

What happened in the memory?

_____
_____
_____

You could list or draw 1–3 things that help you feel calm, safe, or okay when you're lonely.

- People
- Activities
- Places
- Objects

1. _____

2. _____

3. _____

Why not write a kind message to yourself?

Imagine what the person you miss might say if they could comfort you.

Dear me,

Even though I miss being with friends, I know I won't always feel this sad. I am learning how to heal. I am strong, and I'm loved. And that's enough for today.

Signed

_____

Helping Others Helps You

When you're feeling sad or lonely because someone you love has moved on, it can sometimes feel like there's nothing you can do to make things better. But here's something that might surprise you: helping someone else can actually help you feel better, too.

You might be thinking, 'How can helping someone else help me? I'm the one who's sad!' This is a good question. The truth is, when you do something kind for someone else, even something small, it can make your heart feel a little warmer and lighter. It's like sharing a torch with someone in the dark: you both get to see more clearly, and you don't feel so alone. When we're lonely, it's easy to feel stuck inside our own sadness. Helping others may help you step outside of those heavy feelings, even if only for a little while. It gives us a chance to make someone else smile, and when they smile, it can help us smile.

Acts of kindness don't have to be big. Small things can make a big difference. Each time you do something nice, it's like planting a tiny flower in your heart, and sometimes in someone else's heart, too. You might be surprised how it changes how you feel. It can also remind us that we're not the only ones who have a heavy heart. You may be surprised that they also have problems. It's possible that they're lonely too, or perhaps something more. Sometimes we get caught up in our own loneliness that we don't see that the people around us might also be sad, lonely, or hurting, even if they don't say it out loud. When you show kindness, it can knock down walls and, most of all, matter. Please take a step back and watch out for your happy friends or people around you.

Let's talk about Nyxa. When her mother first went into the hospital due to the unfortunate car accident in chapter five, Nyxa had to live with Mary in the Home. There were other children, but she spiralled into loneliness because she missed her mum so much. Then one day, she was sitting on the garden step by herself with an uneaten biscuit in one hand. Her head bowed in silence, she didn't feel like eating. She was lost in thought about how her world had been turned upside-down.

Another girl, Olivia, watched her from the living room window. She sensed how Nyxa was feeling. She saw a reflection of her own pain and loneliness looking back at her. She took the courage to walk outside and sat beside her without saying a word. Yes, that's right, that's what real courage is, because it's not easy to approach someone who's hurting. It took a minute or so for Olivia to break the silence, "Those biscuits are terrible, aren't they? Would you like to try this?" she asked, gently presenting a bar of chocolate to her.

A gliding exchange of snacks. No words spoken, but a lot was said.

That small gesture turned into friendship. Nyxa still really missed her mum, but she started to feel a little better. Olivia moved along her path to healing, too, knowing she could make someone else's day a little brighter. They helped each other get through loneliness, even if it was just a little glimmer of light in their lives. (This is discussed further in section:

Impermanence).

Sometimes, helping can also mean sharing your story.

You don't have to tell everyone everything. But if you feel ready, telling someone, 'I know what it's like to miss someone,' can help them feel understood. It isn't your responsibility to fix their sadness; you just have to listen or be there for them. Helping is a very kind and powerful gift. Please use it. You'll be surprised what you're capable of, even when you're lonely. And here's something else to remember: helping others doesn't mean you have to be perfect or pretend to be happy all the time. You can help and still have sad days. You can be kind and still grieve. You're learning how to carry your dark feelings, while also building something new: hope, connection, and care for others.

Kindness is like a boomerang; when you throw it out into the world, it often comes back to you. You may notice that when you do something kind, someone smiles at you, says thank you, or hugs you a little tighter. And when this happens, your own heart receives a bit of the comfort and love it's been missing.

4. When Someone Blames You

Before we talk about the primary focus of this section, let's talk about being blamed for something you've done. Better to set this straight here.

It was me!

Suppose you did the thing you're being blamed for. If you held your hand up and apologised, let me say… You did the best thing you could have done. People will give you more respect for accepting responsibility for your actions. Sometimes, the person you say 'sorry' to doesn't accept your apology. That's alright too. You were brave enough to admit you did something wrong. By taking ownership, you've learnt that your actions can hurt other people.

Always try to ask yourself, would I like them to do it to me?

Being thick-skinned is a myth. We all hurt!

When something really sad or terrible happens, or a loved one or pet has passed away, an adult may look for someone to blame. This is confusing, as they begin to question what's happened, so grief gets mixed up in their mind with guilt, possibly because they're angry they couldn't prevent it. As they're feeling like this and heartbroken, some people (and I'm sorry to say – parents or other adults) say things that aren't true. Maybe you were told it was your fault they died, or maybe they even shouted, so everyone heard. Perhaps they kept repeating it. And now, that voice is stuck in your head, going around and around.

If this happened to you, I want you to listen to me very carefully:

It's not your fault.

Even if someone said it was.
Even if they looked you in the eye and blamed you.
Even if you've been thinking:

'But… what if I did something different?'
No matter what happened, you aren't to blame.
Pause for a second and please say it very slowly:

'I'm not to blame.'

When someone dies, especially someone close like a parent, a brother, a sister, or even a twin (like poor Aeona), it can feel like the whole world breaks apart. Nothing makes sense anymore. People often struggle to cope with all that pain. Sometimes, instead of feeling sad, they become angry. And instead of crying or asking for help, they point their pain at someone else, and that someone might be you.

Maybe your mum said something like, 'It's your fault your dad is gone,' or 'You should have been watching your brother.' It wasn't said with words, but you feel it in the way they looked at you, or the way they stopped talking to you... Rejected you, even though no one's explained what it was. Aeona did the right thing to say what had happened: there was no shame in that. This very raw moment hurt Aeona so much. It's probably the worst thing a person can do to a child or to someone who's vulnerable.

Let me tell you something about Aeona's mum, Anwen. I'm not making any excuses for the way she blamed her daughter, as it was wrong on so many levels... but some people act irrationally without thinking about who they're hurting. Anwen was hit with so much mental and emotional pressure that she broke. Here, sadly, I'm including the extract so that you can read it from another perspective.

Aeona had just finished another round in the CT scanner to check her skull fracture when they rolled her back into the unit. A sudden pain stabbed at her temple which caused her to wince.

"Sorry, we'll have you settled in a minute," a nurse said. They slid her into bed and began to plug her back into the main monitors when the next sharp pain thrust her into reality. Her pupils dilated, and blood drained from her face. The memory of the explosion hit

her: vivid images… *toilet, spare room, stairs, Jinx, pain, hissing, smell, FLASH!*

"NO!" she screamed.

She couldn't grasp the chronology, but the shocking fact she couldn't deny was that it had happened. There was no doubt

about that, and the purity of her heart came flooding out.

"No! I'm…" she sobbed, burying her head in her hands.

"I'm sorry, Mum. I'm sorry, I'm sorry, Mum."

Anwen quickly rushed to her side. "It's okay. It's okay… I'm here Aeo… I'm here! There's nothing to be sorry for! I'm here!" her mother comforted, unsure of where to touch or pat for all the bandages. She softly wrapped her arms around the distraught girl. "It wasn't your fault. Sometimes, things happen, and we cannot stop them. You can't blame yourself."

"But it was my fault!" she wailed, beating the bedsheet and pounding her knees. "Why did I? Why did I?" She struck her legs harder, her voice growing louder with each cry. "Why?" she begged, her voice breaking. The nurses tried to intervene and prevent the girl from ripping at the wires.

"Shh, my love, it's okay," Anwen whispered to her inconsolable daughter, trying to put more pressure into her hug while conscious of the bandages. "Shh… Shh… Shh," she continued, rocking back and forth. "It's okay! It's Okay!" Anwen couldn't hold back her tears any longer and let them flood down onto Aeona. It had felt so long since she had held her daughter. The sound of 'Shhhhhh!' drowned out the machines.

Then, Aeona pushed back with a look of earnestness and asked bluntly, "Where are Christopher and Daddy?"

"I... I..." stammered Anwen, "I... don't know what to say, Aeona," she cried. "But... but... they're gone, my love."

She knew there was no way her father or her brother would have left her in the hospital all this time without rushing to her side. "Gone?" she asked, wanting to hear the words. "Gone?" she repeated.

Anwen swallowed, lowering the hands that shielded her face. The slow intake of air failed to calm her constricted chest. The words screamed in her mind; the pain of saying the reality reverberated in her throat. "They're gone... Daddy, Chris, the house... everything, Aeona. Gone!"

Aeona screwed up her face in confusion. "Gone? Gone where?"

Anwen didn't want to break it to her like this, but there was no other way. "The house went on fire; that is why you're wrapped in bandages. Don't you remember?" she sobbed. "They.... they... d... didn't make it out!"

She stared at her feet jutting from beneath the blanket as if they belonged to someone else. Her lips parted, but no sound came. A thin thread of unnoticed saliva trembled at her chin. The world pressed in, shrinking to the roar in her ears. Her heart battered at her ribs, a scream she couldn't quiet. "But... who

will feed Jinx?" she stuttered.

The machines beeped on.

The question threw her mother off guard. "Oh, I'm so sorry, Aeo," wept her mother. "But, Jinx... I'm sorry, he's gone too." She mumbled, placing a hand on the girl's foot. "It's going to be okay. It's going to be okay." That was all Anwen could add.

"It's not okay! Christopher and Daddy would be here if I..." she paused, "If I... never went downstairs," she cursed, pulling her foot sharply away from her mother's hand. She then looked directly into Anwen's eyes. "I... I..." she said, hating every word. "I stood... on Jinx... and made the cooker go on."

"Jinx? What? I don't understand, Aeo," her mother asked in confusion. "What has Jinx got to do with the cooker? What do you mean, cooker?" She sat up, trying to see the connection, remembering that the fire inspectors had said it was a gas explosion, a leak or something, most likely from the cooker. "Sorry, did you say... cooker?"

The anger returned to the little girl. Her hands half over her face, she sobbed deeply. Raw emotion turned physical in self-hatred, her fists slamming the mattress in blame, but this time, her mother didn't stop her. She sat and watched in disbelief. The nurses ran over as fast as they could upon seeing the commotion.

Anwen quickly stood up, facing the child. "Do you even understand what you've done?" she questioned, forgetting she was just a mere child... her daughter! "Your dad, Christopher! They... they're gone, Aeona, GONE because of you! How could you?"

The girl shrieked uncontrollably. "Mummy, please... I didn't mean to... They can't be gone?"

Anwen lowered her gaze, lost in the moment. "Sorry, doesn't fix this! It doesn't bring them back! If you'd just stayed out of the kitchen..."

Do you think Anwen was emotionally ready for what Aeona told her?

The clear answer is NO! However, adults, particularly parents, should be able to reason. I'm also sorry to tell you that if either one of the characters had died, the other would have lived. Whether it was Thomas or Christopher, do you think Anwen's response would have been different? Clearly... sadly, no. Aeona would still have been blamed for what was an apparent accident.

Now let's think about what happened to Nyxa and her mother. Could we also blame her for hurting her mother?

"She was twelve, standing in the kitchen. Her mother hunched over at the counter, shielding herself from her father's cruel words, the ghost-like sound of slaps, the dull thuds of fists. Nyxa had grown numb to it over the years. Her sister, Ashley, had left her to the violent wolf. Nyxa didn't think; she just acted. She grabbed the keys from the side, shoved her mother into the car, and slammed the door. Then ran around to the other side and jumped into the driver's seat. She didn't know how to drive, but had observed the monster on many occasions. The adrenaline surged through her, in a wild, reckless need to escape as she turned the key.

Her father already got his second wind and was pounding on the bonnet, screaming vile curses for her to stop, his voice barely audible over the blood rushing in her ears. In an instant, she slammed her foot on the accelerator and with a screech of tyres, her world changed forever. The car lurched into the street. The truck driver didn't have time to react. He slammed into the side of the car with terrifying force. The deafening impact of twisted metal sliced through the saloon like a butter knife. Bones shattered as the car split into two. Time stopped, her world spun, as the crash consumed everything around her. When she opened her eyes, she was in the hospital, alone. Her mother was paralysed from the neck down, her spine was shattered, and she was unable to move or care for herself. Ashley nowhere to be seen. Nyxa was left with nothing but the wreckage of her past, broken and lost, just like the twisted metal of the car."

Was it an accident? We could say it wasn't, but when people panic, they act without thinking. Nyxa needed to get her mother away from her father as quickly as possible. Did she act like anyone would have? Of course, most teenagers would have done exactly the same. It wasn't planned; blind panic got in the way. Her mother never blamed her; she knew she was doing everything she could to save her. Sometimes the consequences of our actions can be brutally harsh. Was Ashley, Nyxa's sister, to blame for leaving? Again, we must say no. She didn't want to leave her mother or sister, but she came to the point that she couldn't take the abuse any longer.

'Blame' is a very complicated word, and with it comes guilt. Some teenagers carry it like a heavy rucksack. And even though no one can see it, it weighs them down every single day. The first thing you need to do is let go of the guilt you carry. It doesn't belong to you. You didn't ask to be blamed, and you certainly didn't earn it, so it's not yours to hold.

5. Big Feelings Are Normal

Have you ever felt so much all at once that you didn't know how to explain it? Maybe you felt sad, angry, scared, numb, or all of these at the same time. When someone blames you for something or when you carry guilt inside your chest, your feelings can get all tangled up like a big knot. This can feel unfair, confusing, and exhausting. But here's what I want you to understand: these feelings are entirely normal.

When something painful happens, or when you're blamed unfairly, your heart goes through a storm. It's natural to feel anger at the person who blamed you, at yourself, or even at the world.

You might feel sad about what was lost.
You may feel confused because things don't seem to make sense.
You might feel guilty, even if you didn't do anything wrong.
You might not feel anything at all. It doesn't mean you're cold or broken; it just means your heart is protecting itself,
like a tortoise pulling itself into its shell.

These huge emotions can come suddenly, or they can sneak up quietly. A song, a smell, a place, or even a memory can bring everything rushing back. One second, you're fine, the next you're overwhelmed. This is grief, this is trauma, and this is what it looks like when your heart is trying to heal.

Sometimes people think they have to be 'tough' and not show their feelings. They try to keep everything locked up inside. But feelings don't go away just because you hide them. They wait. And when they come out, it's often even harder to handle. Being 'tough' doesn't mean pretending you're okay. Please don't pretend; you're only hurting yourself.

You may be asking yourself, how could Aeona not blame herself, with her mum's words scolding, yelling, and screaming… questioning?

"Do you even understand what you've done? GONE because of you! How could you?"

People shouldn't blame anyone based on emotions. It's not fair. Sadly, in the heat of the moment, people don't think, and as in the case of Aeona, we can really hurt those we love. When Aeona said sorry, she said it from a 'guilt-perspective' viewpoint. She'd already blamed herself. She instantly felt a mix of remorse and guilt. This is normal because she's young, she held her hand up and said it was her. This is also because she has a kind heart and was always told to tell the truth.

'Sorry' is the biggest word you'll ever have to use, and even harder saying it to YOURSELF!

If you're angry, try screaming into a pillow. At times, it may be the only way to drown out the hurtful words swimming around your head.

Aeona felt these big feelings too. After the accident, her guilt, sadness, and confusion came crashing down on her all at once. Her heart was trying to process something huge, and the only thing that made sense was that it was her fault. Some people around you can be very hurtful by not understanding your feelings, saying you're being too sensitive. If someone says this to you, know that they're wrong. You're allowed to feel exactly how you feel; it's what you do with your emotions that matters.

Try saying this to yourself:

"I'm allowed to feel whatever I feel."
"My emotions are valid, and I don't have to hide what I'm going through."

Just start slow.

6. Taking Responsibility
Without Beating Yourself Up

Taking responsibility means being honest with yourself about your actions and accepting the consequences. It means owning up to the things you've done, not just to please someone else, but because it helps you grow. This doesn't mean blaming yourself for things you didn't do or agreeing with hurtful things others say about you. It means standing up for yourself, saying, "Yes, I made a mistake."

If you've ever said, "It was me," and truly meant it, this was brave. Taking responsibility is a sign of strength, not a sign of weakness. Especially when the mistake you made had consequences that hurt someone else, saying sorry might not fix everything, but it shows that you care. It also shows that you understand your actions matter and that you're willing to improve.

But here's where it gets tricky: some people confuse taking responsibility with punishment.

You might say sorry over and over, hoping it'll take away the guilt or make people like you again. You hold on to the shame, like a scar, thinking you deserve to wear it forever. This isn't what responsibility's about. Aeona felt ashamed of her actions… the feeling of guilt was there for all to see. The truth was, no one saw her scars as guilt and blamed her. But she did, every time she looked in the mirror at the burns on her face. True responsibility includes forgiveness. It includes forgiving yourself because mistakes don't make you unworthy or mean you're a bad person. It means we sometimes do things, and sometimes they have consequences.

So, we make mistakes, learn from them, and grow.

Think about the difference between saying "I'm the worst" and saying "I made a bad choice." One puts you down and locks you into guilt, the other opens a door for improvement. Aeona believed the accident was her fault. She kept saying, "I'm sorry," and blaming herself. But what she needed, more than anything, was someone to help her see that she had value beyond that mistake. Taking responsibility also doesn't mean hurting yourself emotionally by replaying the event over and over in your head. Once you've acknowledged what happened, apologised if needed, and thought about how to avoid it in the future, you've done what you can. The next step is to let it go.

Sometimes, you might say sorry, and the person you've hurt still doesn't forgive you. That's hard. It can feel like your apology wasn't enough, or that you'll never be free of what happened. But you can't control how someone else responds; you can only control what you do.

Ask yourself:

> *What did I do?*
> *Why did it happen?*
> *What would I do differently next time?*

These questions help you reflect and move forward. Some teenagers worry that if they admit they were wrong, people will use it against them or judge them. However, the truth is that honesty earns respect far more than denial or excuses. You don't need to be perfect to be respected; you need to be real.

7. Making Amends
Fixing What You Can

Now that you've started to understand your feelings and taken responsibility for mistakes, the next step is about making things right. This is called making amends. It means doing something kind, honest, or helpful to show that you're sorry, not just with your words, but with your actions too.

Sometimes, saying "I'm sorry" is enough. However, at other times, people may need more than words. If you broke something, can you help fix it? If you hurt someone's feelings, can you do something kind to show them you care? Making amends is like helping to heal a cut you didn't mean to cause. You can't erase what happened, but you can help the healing process begin.

Here's something important to remember: making amends is about showing, not proving. You don't have to prove that you're a good person; you already are. You're just trying to show that you care, that you've learned, and that you want to make things better.

Let's say you got angry and yelled at your friend. Saying sorry is a great first step. However, you could also write them a kind note or check in on them later. Small actions can mean a lot.

Or if you told a lie and someone got hurt, maybe you can be extra honest in the future and gently let them know you're working on being better. Sometimes, the person you want to say sorry to might not want to talk to you. That's okay. You can still make amends in your own way. Write a letter, even if you don't send it. Every kind act increases the good in you, and this matters more than you know.

Aeona couldn't undo what had happened; sometimes, what happened, whether it was a broken vase, a torn picture, or a broken heart, couldn't be fixed, but maybe a relationship of trust and honesty could be. Telling the truth about it is a huge thing to do. Even if the person, as painful as it is, doesn't show you forgiveness.

We'll never know the outcome of blame, guilt, redemption, and forgiveness if we don't try.

'Will Anwen give her daughter a hug?' And 'Will Aeona forgive herself and let go?' I hope so.

You might be scared and asking yourself, 'What if I don't know how to fix it?' This is normal. It takes courage to try. Start small by saying to the person, "I've been thinking about what happened, and I feel bad. I want to make things right." There are two possible outcomes: either the person isn't ready to forgive, and they might even explode in your face again, repeating the hurt and blame. Yes, this can seem like a step backward, but your heart has cleaned itself; this is about you doing the right thing, not forgiveness.

I want to tell you everything's going to work out fine, but sometimes we have to walk away to protect ourselves. Just like you're learning, the people around you are learning too. Sometimes they'll be ready to forgive and accept your amends. Sometimes they won't. But that doesn't mean your efforts don't count. What matters is that you tried.

Stop thinking, 'I wish I could go back,' because you can't; you can only move forward.

Small changes make a big difference.

You've read, understood, and reflected on the guilt you carry for mistakes, but now we're coming to the end of this section, see how the word has started to release its hold on you.

GUILT… Guilt… guilt… guilt… guilt… guilt…

You've also faced your feelings, taken responsibility, and are now going to try to make things better; now you're ready to give your heart some peace. As Aeona's story unfolds, we can see that she still has a lot of pain, fear, and blame to overcome. But in time, she'll see that her life didn't end with the accident. She has more love to give, more dreams to grow, and more life to live. You do too.

8. Understanding Addiction

Addiction can affect anyone, including teenagers. It's not just about drugs or alcohol. It involves anything from vaping and gaming to social media, food, or gambling. What starts as a way to feel good, fit in, or escape stress can slowly take control of your life. For many of you, recognising when a habit crosses the line into addiction can be difficult.

Understanding what it is, how it develops, and what you can do if you're struggling or worried about someone else is very important. If you, yourself, feel you're addicted to something, there's no shame in holding your hand up. Please be brave; no one's going to judge you, especially nowadays with so many addictive things around. Whether your concern is about substance use or compulsive behaviours, we're going to go through a number of them to gain some insight and offer support to help you come to terms with it. First, let's see if we can lessen its hold on you.

So, what is addiction, or what does it mean to be an addict? The textbook definition describes it as a condition where a person loses control or overuses something despite the negative consequences. It affects the brain's reward system, making your body and mind crave a substance or activity to feel normal. Over time, this craving can overpower everything, from logic and relationships to health and responsibilities.

There are two broad types of addiction.

Substance addiction includes alcohol, nicotine, soft drugs, prescription medications, and hard drugs like cocaine or ecstasy. And behavioural addiction, which involves compulsive acts, such as excessive gaming, online scrolling, eating, or even exercise. It usually develops gradually with just a little of it. Perhaps you were pressured into doing something by your peers, or you just felt bored and wanted something to take your mind off it. At first, they'll bring pleasure, relief, and a sort of escapism from the reality around you. But once, twice, three times, a pattern starts to form, and your brain begins to depend on it. Tolerance builds up; once more doesn't quite have the same effect as before, so you either increase the amount, and before you know it, every time you stop, it causes you to have withdrawal symptoms, such as anxiety, irritability, or physical discomfort.

Not everyone who uses a substance or engages in an activity becomes addicted. Some teenagers can stop doing what they're doing, but others will delve deeper and deeper, wanting more and more. Please, don't test yourself at this; it's a dare with no winners.

"I'm not addicted. I can stop at any time."

You may notice that it starts to interfere with schoolwork, relationships, mental wellbeing, or daily life. If you or your friends begin to see a change, it's time to take it seriously. But when you start to crave the next fix, even your friends might find it difficult to stop you, and you know where this is going. Especially when you start to hide it, lie about using, or withdraw from others and push them away, a domino effect happens, one after the other. Addictive behaviour thrives in secrecy. The longer you keep it hidden, the more control it has over your choices, mood, and how you take care of yourself. Stop for a minute and think. If you say, "I'm not addicted," do you really know the signs? I truly hope you can recognise the early hints: they're essential for preventing long-term damage, and reaching out is a brave first step towards recovery and a better understanding of how these things work.

Supporting science

Let's examine some of the science behind addiction. There are a number of factors which can cause it. It develops from a mix of things: biological, psychological, and environmental influences. Understanding the reasons behind having an addiction can help you respond with empathy and awareness, without judgment from others and, most of all, yourself.

Biological factors include your genetics and brain chemistry. You may be more vulnerable to addiction because of inherited traits from family members. The brain's reward system, which releases a chemical called dopamine, may respond more strongly to certain substances or behaviours. Once you start to repeat the action, it begins to shape your behaviour and makes your body put the substance into its 'needs' category. This 'repeat-stop-repeat' routine is a tough one to break, because it's like being hungry or thirsty. When you feel a little pain in your stomach, your body's sending out a signal that it wants food; a dry tongue and a tired breath mean your brain's telling you that you need to drink. It's just the same for your addictive trait; when it's been programmed into your daily routine, these patterns are complicated to reverse.

Psychological influences can involve your underlying mental wellbeing, such as anxiety, depression, ADHD, and trauma, to name but a few. Another is that some teenagers may use it like medicine, instead of taking tablets. It may seem better in some ways, but as with everything, too much of anything isn't the best approach. It only generally masks or puts off addressing the issue. For example, if you have anxiety, you might turn to cigarettes or vaping to feel calm. Others might use excessive gaming or binge eating as a distraction from emotional pain. Unfortunately, the addictive relief is only temporary and often increases your distress and dependence on the stimuli. Where you live, your school, and your street may also contribute to the vicious circle. Environmental factors, such as being with people who are probably addicted themselves, is a troublesome place to be. When a little try turns into just one more go, it gets hold of you. Sorry for the cliché, but maybe you've heard of 'monkey do, monkey say.'

When Aeona was trying to find the library in Chapter 27, she asked a girl behind the counter in the garage, Chloe. She was like any other girl: bored, lonely, or troubled. She got swept up in the "everyone else is doing it" mindset. It doesn't take much to get drawn into something. Fortunately, she crossed paths with Officer Megan. This encounter could've gone the wrong way, but Megan saw that Chloe was just going through a tough time. Sometimes, addictions can lead to teenagers hanging around causing a nuisance, random petty theft, or being rude to people around them.

If you don't have any other outlets for stress or emotional pain, most teenagers push themselves into addictive behaviours as coping mechanisms. Plus, living with others who say, "I'm not addicted!" is a very tough place to be. To make matters worse, the lack of any support or guidance makes it even harder to find a way out.

Media and advertising can glamorise substance use and risky behaviour, making it seem exciting or harmless. Repeated exposure to these messages, especially online, through banners, pop-ups, and ads, can influence your choices more than you realise. Big advertising companies have done their psychological research: they know how to hit you with everything they've got. To add to the onslaught, seeing influencers or celebrities use something without disclosing its darker side can send misleading signals about what's safe and what's not, or even normalise it.

It isn't about having a weakness or making bad decisions. It's often about trying to survive or feel better in a world that feels overwhelming. When you understand the deeper roots of your addiction, you can focus less on blame and more on finding ways to lessen addictive traits.

How does it affect you?

Addiction impacts every area of your life: physically, emotionally, socially, and mentally, as discussed above. The effects often overlap, reinforcing the cycle and making recovery feel difficult. Understanding the full impact of how it can interfere with your wellbeing and daily routines can help you see why it's important to get early and consistent help. This is a catch-22 situation; you're reading this, and now you see, it's probably already too late. I know this sounds negative, but the road to getting yourself sorted out is to say, 'I have to do something, this is becoming too much!'

Please watch out for yourself and your friends; try to think about something more meaningful before getting caught in a cycle of doing, regret, repeating, and regret.

The harsh reality is that it creates a rollercoaster of emotions: the intense highs followed by deep lows. Mood swings, irritability, guilt, and sadness are common. Over time, it can become overwhelming and, in the end, you start to feel numb, hopeless, or unable to enjoy life without the addictive behaviour or substance.

If you're addicted to technology, we all are to some degree, it'll cloud your ability to think clearly and make sound decisions. Think about it: how many seconds does it take between your phone beeping and you picking it up, if it's not already in your hand? I know you're reading this, but how far away is your phone from you right now? You can't deny that you would've glanced beside yourself right now, or paused for a minute to look at the screen. If it was less than ten seconds, we may have a little problem. You might also find that it gets in the way of concentrating in school, remembering homework, or staying organised in virtually anything.

Using AI excessively may also be added to the list of

what's considered to be an addiction. But, "I only use it to answer difficult questions or to make it easier to understand!" is what has just flashed through your mind. The simple answer is that you don't, but you're intelligent and creative. If you put your mind to it, you can learn and improve on your own. It's true that AI is a fantastic tool; I'm not denying this. However, over-reliance is the issue. Your creativity and motivation will suffer.

One more thing about using AI before we move on. Type a question into AI and watch how your brain and body react when you press Enter. You'll see a peak in dopamine, a chemical that gives you a feeling of pleasure and satisfaction. However, it's not the same feeling when you're working hard at something and suddenly you figure it out. You did it. But, AI completely cuts out the 'Eureka' moment, and you're not letting your brain or yourself have the "I did it, all by myself," reward you really need.

Let's think about your friends and family for a second, because socially, addiction can put a wedge in

your relationship with them.

Once you start to become addicted, you may start to lie, push people away, or begin to choose the 'quick-fix' over a meaningful connection. If this happens, it can break down the trust they have in you, and as feelings of isolation grow, you're drawn more into the addiction. Then the little voice in your head wins, and it happily starts to shape your identity. It wants to have the last word: "You don't need them, you've got me," and by this time, it already has its claws dug deep into your mind. But this version of you isn't the whole truth. Addiction is something you're experiencing; it doesn't mean this is who you are.

I want to say I'm proud of you for wanting to do this. It isn't an easy step to take. It takes a lot of courage, and without sugar coating, it'll be very tough, requiring patience and honesty. You'll be knocked down a few times, but you'll rise above it. Why? Because you've done the hardest thing; you've acknowledged that there's an issue, it's causing you harm, and you want to have a go at taking some of your life back, even if you still enjoy doing it. Having inner conflict is normal, and the first step, if possible, is to identify the needs and triggers and write down what's happening. Do you remember how it started and what role it plays in your life?

Once you've identified your patterns, consider replacing the addictive behaviour with alternatives. This doesn't mean trying to distract yourself with just anything. It means finding things that genuinely help you process your emotions, stress, or boredom. For example, if you turn to vaping when you feel anxious, try replacing that habit with… chewing gum. It's generally not the what, but in rewiring your brain to look at something else. The continuous motion of chewing distracts your brain with the same relief, stimulation, or comfort that the substance used to provide. Chewing becomes a surprisingly powerful tool for breaking the cycle for several reasons. You're old enough to understand that it'll cause problems with your teeth, but it's a lesser evil in the broader scheme of things. Tooth decay vs addiction, a tough one to address, but you've got a choice: sugar vs sugar-free. There's generally always an alternative.

The physical redirection gives the mouth and jaw something to do, which can satisfy the need for oral stimulation. This is especially helpful if you're addicted to smoking or vaping, where the act of putting something in the mouth becomes part of the habit. Chewing gum, crunchy snacks, or even a toothpick can physically interrupt that urge and keep the hands and mouth busy. It becomes a sensory trick that shifts focus. This slight shift in attention can help delay or weaken the craving. Chewing is a repetitive and rhythmic activity that can help calm the nervous system and give the mind something else to focus on, even if only for a few minutes. Additionally, using the muscles in your jaw can help alleviate some of the stress you may be experiencing. Some people use chewing as a way to practise mindfulness, especially when trying to ground themselves during intense cravings. Paying attention to the texture, taste, and rhythm of chewing can bring you back into the present. This can make you pause and make a conscious choice instead of acting on the little voice in your head.

You're a teenager, so you'll probably think this isn't for you, but breathing exercises, in through your nose and out through your mouth, can help at the time of the craving or when you start to feel the sudden urge to reach for your addiction. It's something to do in the now, strong deep breaths… big ones, like you're sucking all the air in the room in through your nose. This causes the brain to be overloaded with the sensation of the rushing air, to the point that it feels you're going to give yourself brain freeze.

It's about the distraction rather than the act.

It's the same for the below and all the other self-help tricks… that's what they are: tricks. As your mind can play tricks on you sometimes, try to do the same with it: fool it into thinking, believing, or understanding something different from what it wants, rather than letting it control your actions. If you're into music, listen to your favourite song. Depending on where you live, you can go for a walk, go to the gym, even up and down your stairs, or around your home.

Suppose gaming or scrolling online is the addiction. It's okay to spend some time enjoying social media to stay informed about current events and trends, but please set aside some structured downtime. I know it'll be difficult to put your device down once you're on it, but try to set an alarm and stick to it: easier said than done, I know. If you say to yourself, "Just five more minutes," or "Just one more game," you're losing your fight. An alarm is probably the best option, because if you ask a friend or parent to remind you after one or two hours, it'll start a conflict. It's like you're fighting with yourself to stop, but you don't want to, and then those supporting you come into the firing line. Then it's trench warfare, and then the shouting starts again…

"Hey, it's been two hours, would you like to do something else?"
"No, go away. I've only been on it for fifteen minutes."
"Leave me alone, I'm just finishing this level."

Finding a replacement isn't easy if you're addicted to something, because whatever it is will probably seem boring as it won't give you the same adrenaline rush or excitement as the addiction. But with repetition, your brain can adapt to new ways of finding relief. Keep telling yourself, "I can do this," and please also try to build routines: addiction thrives in chaos and impulsivity, so having regular times for waking up, eating, exercising, studying, and resting gives your brain some stability. Try starting your day with a simple goal, like making your bed or having a little workout. Later in the day, set an alarm to eat dinner at a specific time. Yes, these all sound silly, but your body clock will kick in and start to control what you do at any particular time. This will push the urges and boredom aspects to the side lines as you begin to regain control. Most importantly, don't be hard on yourself at first. There'll be days when you slip, but this doesn't mean you've failed. Ask yourself what happened, how you felt, and what you can do to help next time. Speak gently to yourself, with encourage- ment and hope. Choosing self-help doesn't mean you're doing it alone, because no one's got your back. It's about taking an active role in weaning yourself off the addictive thing. Support from others, like friends and family, will hopefully steer you in the right direction. If they've lost complete trust in you, for whatever reason, it might be time to speak to a professional, like a counsellor or maybe a teacher. It ultimately starts with you, your decisions, and please be honest with yourself.

If you're reading this because you've got a friend who's struggling with addiction, I understand it can be incredibly difficult, especially when you care about them. The most important thing to do is to approach the situation with empathy, not judgment. Remember, their addiction is stronger than your friendship!

Let your friend know you've noticed some changes and that you're concerned, not because you want to control them, but because you want them to be safe and supported. Start the conversation gently. You might say something like, "I've noticed you've been using a lot lately. Is there anything I can help with?" or "I care about you and just want to understand what's going on." Try not to accuse or label them. Keep the focus on how you feel and what you've observed, rather than making assumptions about their behaviour. Your friend will probably deny the issue, become defensive, or try to push you away. I told you so! This is often a result of shame, fear, or a lack of readiness to face the truth. Be patient. Let them know you're available if and when they do want to talk. Check in regularly and try to spend time together doing things unrelated to the addiction. Depending on how far in they are, it can be just as hard for you as it is for them. Hopefully, you can catch them before they spiral out of control by being present in their life without pushing too hard.

It was one of the main reasons Ashley, Nyxa's sister, left home. Ash was addicted to something; let's not talk about it here, but it caused a rift between her mother and sister. Nyxa loved her dearly and couldn't bear to watch what it was doing to herself. She'd on many occasions talked quietly to her, but it had come to the point where Ash wasn't listening or refused to listen. This shows how far into the addiction she'd been pulled. Please do what you can and give support. Most of all, let them know you're there for them.

If you're the one who has an issue of being addicted, there are so many helplines where you can speak to counsellors, doctors, or support services. I've included an extensive list of global helplines at the back of this book. If your addiction involves a device, you may want to visit the website for some ideas. It may at least distract you, even for a little while, from gaming or social media. If you're not ready to take this step, what about small changes? Avoid brushing off your behaviour by asking a friend to cover up for you or by pretending everything's fine, but also try not to be ashamed or become aggressive if someone gives you a lecture. I know you'll be defensive, but think about it - it may be better to have a couple of people fighting in your corner than to lose their friendship.

Here's a wake-up call.

It may come to the point where your addiction becomes dangerous. Your health deteriorates, you don't eat, you don't speak. You have to realise that you're in a dark hole. They care about you and will help you in every way they can, but it takes a toll on them, too. The pressure of watching the person they love turn into someone else is draining. Now they're hit on all sides, their own mental and emotional wellbeing, and now yours.

You may be stealing or borrowing with no intention of returning, to get your next fix. It might not be a physical thing either. You may become so wrapped up in the addiction that you might start buying things in the games with real money, skins, weapons, or anything else that will make your character level up. For physical addictions it's the same; it's not getting to the next level, but you'll be raising the stakes in gambling, raising the number of drugs or turn from non-alcoholic energy drinks to the real thing. Adults or friends will have to either forcefully remove the addiction or take further action. Whatever they do, they're doing it in your best interests and for your own safety. It might feel like betrayal, but in truth, it's one of the strongest acts of care and friendship they can give.

9. When to Get Professional Help

There are times when addiction becomes too overwhelming to manage on your own. When it begins affecting your ability to function, when you feel helpless, out of control, or unable to stop despite serious consequences (as we've discussed), it's essential to reach out for professional help. This doesn't mean you've failed. It means you're strong enough to recognise when you need more support.

Professional help can come in many forms. I know how you feel, but please start with a teacher you trust. Remember, any adult in a school is required by law to inform the counsellor if they're concerned. They should listen without judgement and can guide you towards the right kind of support. They might not have the knowledge to help you directly, but they'll let your parents know who to talk to. You probably don't like any of these suggested options, but please don't hesitate to reach out. If talking face-to-face feels too difficult, consider writing a note or message to express your feelings. Someone who cares can hand it to an adult if you're not up for it.

A doctor or mental health professional can also assess the nature of your addiction and recommend a treatment plan that best suits you. It might involve therapy, support groups, medication, or referrals to specialised programmes. Please don't be intimidated by all of this; it's been carefully thought through, and most plans are tailored specifically for you. Talk to a trusted person about what's troubling you. If you're worried about more people finding out, before you speak, ask about confidentiality. But you can't ask the adult to keep it a secret if they feel you're in danger of hurting yourself. Their priority is to help you, not to judge or punish you for whatever you're addicted to.

Recovering from an addiction can take time, but you're not alone; thousands of teenagers come out the other end. It doesn't mean you won't have any setbacks, as some addictions can take longer than others to break. It means learning to respond with new ways of building different habits, which will support your mental and physical health. It begins with this important decision, the first step towards recovery. You might relapse, and no one said it was going to be easy. It can happen, and if it does, it doesn't mean you're back at the beginning. This is normal; give it another shot. You need to make a firm decision to stop or at least get it under control. The cycle can go on and on until you finally beat it. It's a process, not an event. Some days feel easy, others impossibly hard. There will be moments of temptation, frustration, and doubt. There will also be moments of clarity, strength, connection, and joy. Moments where you begin to remember what it feels like to live freely, enjoy sitting with your friends, and have meaningful relationships with those around you.

10. Crushing Hard
Infatuation and Unconditional Love

If you've ever found yourself completely obsessed with a celebrity, thinking about them constantly, watching every interview, and knowing their birthday, favourite colour, and even what kind of dog they have, you're not the only one. Nowadays, every detail of virtually every film star, musician, or sports personality is available on the internet for all to see. Everywhere they go, everything they do, they can't escape the paparazzi and fans that follow them. It's a world they've created for themselves in the limelight, and along with it come the not-so-good things about being famous. For many teenagers, their idols are role models, and sometimes, it goes one step further, you worship the ground they walk on.

Having deep feelings, admiration, or even an emotional attachment to a famous person is something most of us experience at some point. It can be confusing, exciting, overwhelming, and even painful at times. You might even find yourself saying, "I love them," or thinking, "If they only knew me, they'd love me back." These thoughts are pretty normal, especially when you're starting to discover your own feelings and build your own identity.

But what's really going on when you're head-over-heels for someone you've never actually met? Is it real love? Is it healthy, or is it just a phase?

Being a teenager is a very special milestone; you're no longer a child, but you're not an adult yet. Your brain is still developing, your body is changing at an incredible rate, and your emotions feel all over the place. It's not easy to understand or differentiate your feelings. It's only a matter of time before you start having romantic feelings for another person, and celebrities are often the easiest outlet for these feelings. Why? Because they're everywhere. They're designed to look and sound amazing. You get to see their best moments: polished performances, edited photos, and charming interviews.

You get the illusion of knowing them, even though they don't actually know you. Please note, we're focusing purely on celebrities or influencers here, like on-screen singers, social media influencers, or other personalities, rather than the people around you. We'll discuss the differences between 'unrequited love' and when we fall for a celebrity in the next section, which is known as a parasocial relationship: a one-sided emotional bond you form with someone who isn't in your life... directly. This doesn't matter to you, as the feeling is real and you're not "making it up" or being silly. It depends on how much you perceive you love them. I know you might not like to hear this… but you need to recognise that they aren't your friend. Your feelings are valid; their music is relatable, as if the lyrics were written just for you. To you, the connection is real.

If the celebrity you love feels more than just a fantasy, if they give you butterflies, make you cry, or give you comfort during difficult times, that's okay. In fact, there's a reason it feels this way. Your brain is hard-wired to feel deeply for others. You're growing at an incredible rate, and hormones like dopamine and oxytocin are surging through your body at this stage of life, which makes emotional experiences stronger than they were when you were younger. When you watch your favourite celebrity perform or speak kindly in an interview, your brain might feel the same way it would if you were talking to someone you care about in real life.

If you're struggling at school, with friendship problems, or with family issues, a celebrity can become a kind of escape. Thinking about them might make you feel safer or less alone. You might even imagine conversations with them, or pretend they're someone who would understand and protect you. This is a way of coping with overwhelming emotions and what you're going through. I know it can be tough to hear, but try to stay grounded in the present reality and recognise that the emotional comfort you're feeling is coming from within you, not from an actual relationship with the person.

Singers, actors, and people you see as role models change all the time as new trends come along. Straight onto your screen, the internet has made your world a much smaller space. The fantastic tool you have in your hand most of the time provides you with access to the diversity and beauty of everyone on the planet. So many beautiful people of different shapes, forms, and languages cross amazing barriers. But now… something is starting to blur our reality even further, and that's AI (Artificial Intelligence). Perfect images are generated at the tap of a button, creating unquestionable beauty and perfection.

Whether you fall for an AI life-like creation, a real person, or even an animated character like in Anime and Manga, it doesn't make the feelings any less real.

Have you ever caught yourself smiling at your screen because of something your favourite anime character said or did? Maybe you've spent time thinking about them, drawing them, writing stories about them, or even imagining what it would be like if they were real. You might even like one of them so much you're becoming infatuated with them, you're not alone. Hurtful people might say horrible things and call you weird. For many teenagers around the world, anime characters become more than just animated drawings. In your mind, they're alive, and you feel connected to them, inspired by them, and comforted by their stories. This is a very real part of growing up and learning about your feelings, your dreams, and even your values. It's great to have some of the characters as role models to follow, as a lot of them have clear moral values.

It all seems so real: their world, their lives, and everything they say. In many cases, they speak directly to you and only you.

But why?

One of the main reasons they're so intense is because of how anime is made. The shows often dive deep into emotions and character development. You don't just see action or comedy; you get to know the characters' backstories, motivations, fears, dreams, and friendships. You might watch them struggle through pain or loss, fight for something they believe in, or care for the people around them. This emotional depth fosters a profound connection within you. Think about it: when you watch a character grow, face challenges, or support others, it can feel like you're going through it with them. You're not just watching them; you're cheering them on, worrying about them, and maybe even seeing part of yourself in their situations. This emotional bond you create is real, even if the character isn't.

Some anime characters are especially popular, and for good reason. For example, you might feel something for Levi from Attack on Titan because of his quiet strength, loyalty, and attitude, or Mikasa Ackerman, who's a complex character known for her exceptional combat skills, fierce loyalty, and quiet strength. Does this sound like anything you can relate to? It's okay because maybe you have no one you can talk to about the emotions you see in anime. Others fall hard for Todoroki Shoto from My Hero Academia, who's mysterious, powerful, and has a complicated backstory that makes him feel deep and genuine. If you like someone fun and outgoing, perhaps Naruto Uzumaki caught your attention for his determination and big heart. It shows that love is possible and you need to be loved, like with Hinata Hyuga, because she's sweet and caring. Each character leaves a mark on you, as well as showing you that relationships can be cross-cultural and cross-continent.

It's not just about how the characters are drawn, but also about the way they look and make you think about yourself. Whether you've fallen for Naruto Uzumaki, Gojo (Jujutsu Kaisen), Usagi, or L from Death Note, you need to remind yourself that all of them have been meticulously crafted, with their own carefully written scripts showing you… the reader, the viewer, that they're gentle, strong, and devoted. The character was designed to be lovable, cool, or sweet. Their dialogue, personality, and even appearance, are all carefully created to make you like them. So, it's no wonder you're drawn to them. You're not weird; you've got a vivid imagination and are developing your sense of emotional identity.

Reading through the above characteristics can reveal a great deal about yourself. You may admire their strength because you want to feel more confident in your own life. Perhaps you're drawn to someone kind and gentle because that's the kind of energy you want in your life. You value the importance of their depth, and your loving heart is only reaching out for a piece of it. Liking a character isn't just about them; it's also about you. Your crush might show you what kind of love or friendship you're hoping to find, what qualities you admire most in others, or how much you care about connection, even if it's in a fantasy space. Instead of feeling embarrassed, try asking yourself: "What does this character tell me about what I want in real life?"

This is where real personal growth happens.

Believe it or not, crushing on an anime character can actually be helpful, as long as it doesn't take over your life. Your feelings can motivate you to be creative, try new things, or reflect on your emotions. For example, your love for a character might inspire you to write stories or fan fiction, learn to draw or create animation clips, or get into voice acting by learning Japanese. This could also develop into storytelling, or make you think more about your own values and relationships. If you're going through a tough time in real life, anime can feel comforting. The character can give you a focus to move forward, representing hope, protection, or kindness when you need it most.

But, like anything, too much of a good thing can get out of balance. It's important to notice if your feelings are making you unhappy or disconnected from your real life. Please keep an eye out for some red flags in the way you react. If you feel sad, lonely, or angry when someone says something hurtful about the character you love, that's where you have to pause for a second. Avoiding real-life friendships or experiences isn't the best way forward. Please don't compare real people with your anime character, or feel disappointed when they don't match or live up to your expectations. Maybe you feel anxious or upset when you can't watch the anime, or feel like no one else could ever make you feel the same way as they do. If any of this sounds familiar, it doesn't mean there's anything wrong with you; it just means your heart might need a break or a bit more balance in your life. It could also be like an addiction, which we discussed earlier in this book.

In Shadows Chant, chapter eight, the two girls, Ava and Masie, loved anime so much that they'd often argue over who was better, Naruto or Sasuke. Other times, they'd get into a discussion about who was better, Natsu or Gray, from Fairy Tail. If you're unfamiliar with these characters, you probably have your own opinion. But in the end, what mattered most was that the two girls shared a passion for each other. When they weren't watching anime or drawing their characters, they found common ground and had real, human conversations.

You can still love the character, but it helps if you gently reconnect with the world around you, too.

The best thing you can do is appreciate the emotions the character brings, while still living fully in your own life. Try to hold onto both things: the love you feel for the character, and the awareness that your real-life story matters even more. Try writing about why you love them, creating something inspired by them, and sharing your thoughts with friends who understand or share the same interest in anime.

Millions of people, of all ages, get emotionally attached to fictional characters, especially in anime. These stories are designed to touch your heart, and your brain is wired to respond. What you're feeling is human.

Having a crush on K-pop idols is no different from having a crush on anime and manga. Korean Pop, if you don't already know, is a genre of popular music originating from South Korea. The singers and dancers are cleverly designed to be deeply appealing, not just because of their talent, but also because of how much content fans get to see. You don't just hear their music; you also watch behind-the-scenes videos, vlogs, live streams, dance practices, interviews, and variety shows. The idols often speak directly to fans… or followers, calling them (even if generally) by name and talking about their own struggles and dreams. This is why it feels like you have an emotional closeness to them… they're real!

You feel connected to the person because they're made to be:

Confident, Mysterious, Artistic,

Charismatic, Goofy, Sweet,

Gentle, Kind, Loyal,

Strong, Energetic, Fearless,

Vulnerable, Bright, Youthful, Fun-loving, Charming.

And because you connected with the star, singer, influencer, or character, it also means that you have many of the above qualities in your wonderful heart, too.

Maybe you're missing a couple of the above in your real life… which is okay. Not having all of them doesn't mean anything is wrong, but it does make your heart feel warm and gives you direction to strive for and even want to build in yourself. It's great to be inspired by your K-pop, just like anime, but sometimes there's a line that you have to, painfully at times, draw. Being upset when they date someone, or thinking your real friends can't compete, or if you're spending more time in their world rather than in real relationships, this is when it helps to pause and check in.

Ask yourself:

'Is this helping me grow?'

'Am I happy with how much time I spend thinking about them?'

'Do I love them because of how they make me feel, or because I think I need them to be happy?'

Falling for a K-pop idol is a powerful, emotional, and meaningful experience. It doesn't make you silly or shallow for doing so; in fact, it shows how capable you are of having deep feelings, loyalty, and creativity. Just like anime or celebrity infatuations, they're part of discovering who you are.

But, there's another thing you need to protect your heart from.

Trends change, and people age, making it inevitable that influencers, like current K-pop singers, do too. Just as they move in their direction, to be replaced by another beautiful person, so must you prepare yourself for the changes. Instead of purely focusing on one person that you like, you must learn to have a buffer zone, where you're ready for any sudden changes. Just as things happen in your life, things happen in theirs, too.

A painful truth

Sadly, sometimes… horrible things happen, and your first reaction is usually shock. You might feel like, "This can't be real," or "There has to be a mistake." If it was a sudden and traumatic death, like a car accident or overdose, it can feel even more unreal. You might refresh social media over and over again, hoping to see a post saying it was fake or just a rumour. This reaction is your body's way of trying to protect itself from the hurt by not accepting the truth right away.

Once the painful reality sinks in, grief and sadness often follow. You might listen to their music, re-watch interviews, or scroll through tribute posts. Your sadness is real, even if the relationship wasn't in-person. You weren't just a fan; you had a deeply personal and emotional connection with them. Maybe they helped you through tough times, made you feel seen, or inspired your creativity. It feels like you've lost a piece of your heart. Many teenagers, like yourself, may also feel confused or angry, especially if the cause of death was self-induced or something that could have been prevented. You might think, "How could this happen to someone so talented?" or "Why didn't someone help them?" Sometimes, there's anger at others for not recognising the signs or not offering help. The media, fake fans, or even your celebrity, for making a choice that led to their death. Grief is messy, and there's no "right" way to feel. If you haven't already, please read through the first section: 'Loss, Bereavement, and Grief' for some kind and caring ways of dealing with such a profound loss.

Fear and Anxiety

If a celebrity has a terrible accident in a crash or from excessive substance abuse that leads to death, some teenagers start to feel anxious about their own safety or the safety of people they care about, because it makes them feel incredibly vulnerable. They were perfect and... just how? In most teenagers' minds, they appear as if they could be immortal, like they could overcome everything. Sadly, my friend, they're no different than you or me. Even anime characters aren't invincible, and at the whim of the creators, writers, or animators, they too can be killed off as part of the developing story and replaced by another character.

You might think, "If it can happen to them, it could happen to anyone." This fear is part of realising how fragile life can be. For some of you reading, it can even trigger panic attacks, nightmares, or a fear of driving, having a good time, or even questioning your own existence. If these feelings become overwhelming… please reach out. If you've felt it, so have other fans like yourself. It's okay to talk to someone you trust, a friend or an adult. Even if you know other fans, grief can make you feel isolated. Try to talk to others who understand what you're going through, whether in forums or communities. Remember, friends who aren't into the same celebrity or genre might not understand why you're so hurt by it all. Some adults might say, "It's just a famous person, why are you so upset?" This can make you feel like you're grieving alone or like your pain doesn't matter. But your feelings are authentic and valid, because losing someone who meant something to you, even though they were on a screen, is still something to feel heartbroken about.

To step forward from the terrible news, you might ask yourself deeper questions about them, like:

What did this person teach me?

How can I live with more purpose?

You might get involved in some of the same causes they cared about, like different charities. This will help you with your own mental well-being by trying some of the following:

Creating fan art or tribute videos

Lighting candles or writing letters

Posting messages or sharing their favourite quotes

Listening to their music or watching their work again

Talking with other fans who understand

This helps you feel connected with the now and what matters, and that's you. It also keeps the good parts of that person alive… the qualities that inspired you and gave you strength at the beginning. Nothing has changed; their values, their morals. Their legacy can still be carried forward, and what they've given you has made you a better, more loving person.

11. Infatuation vs unconditional love

Let's talk about two words that often get mixed up: infatuation and unconditional love. When you're in the middle of a celebrity obsession, like in the previous section, it can feel like the deepest love you've ever felt. You might think, "I love them no matter what," or "I'll always support them." This can feel like unconditional love, but it's essential to look a little deeper.

Infatuation is intense, fast, overwhelming, and often based on fantasy, as it involves a strong desire to be loved. It makes your heart race, and it's all you can think about. But it's not usually based on who the person is; it's based on who you imagine them to be. Let's pause for a minute to reread this.

It's not usually based on who the person is;

it's based on who you imagine them to be.

You're in love with the idea of them, a version you've built in your mind from clips, photos, and performances. Unconditional love, on the other hand, is something that grows over time. It's about truly knowing someone, the good, the bad, the complicated, and still choosing to love them anyway. It requires real-life experiences, emotional honesty, and a mutual connection. This is something you can't have with someone you've never met, like in anime, K-pop, or other celebrities.

So, while your feelings may be strong, they're more likely a form of intense admiration or fantasy-based love, and this is okay. It doesn't make your emotions any less real or less valid; it just means they're happening in a space that's more about imagination than the real world.

If you're someone who cares deeply, is loyal, and is passionate about people who inspire you, it says something good about your emotional depth. If you get emotionally attached to celebrities, you're not weird, too much, or over the top. It often means you're thoughtful, imaginative, empathetic, and capable of forming powerful connections with others. Maybe you're someone who sees beyond the surface of a person. You have a beautiful way of looking beyond the outside and are drawn to a person's inner kindness. This reflects your own values, and you see a shared value. When you say, "I love them for who they are inside," you're also revealing this inside yourself and how it matters to you. And this is important.

Some people may tell you you're being silly or irrational for having feelings about these things. But love, whether it's romantic, emotional, or spiritual, is a very normal and human thing. This is the kind of love that makes you defend someone, care about their well-being, and feel joy at their success. This kind of love is what the world needs more of.

A One-way Love Story: Unrequited Love

Have you ever had a massive crush on someone who didn't like you back? Maybe you've been in love or are in love with a friend, a classmate, or even someone you barely know. You think about them all the time, imagining what it would be like to be together, and hope they notice you. It's as if you don't even exist, or they might not feel the same way. If this sounds familiar, you're not alone. This feeling of one-sided or unrequited love is more common than you think.

Many teenagers experience this, and it can be particularly hurtful. You have strong feelings for someone, but they don't return the feelings. You might dream about being their boyfriend or girlfriend, or they may have feelings for someone else. Sometimes they don't see you that way, or they may not even know how you feel. It can happen with a best friend, someone in your school, or even someone you meet while out. No matter who it is, the pain of loving someone who doesn't love you back can be really intense.

There are different kinds of unrequited love. One type is when you like someone secretly and never tell them. Another is when you tell them and they say they don't feel the same. There's also a third kind, when you are close friends, and you wish it could be something more, but they don't want that. All of these are normal and extremely common. It doesn't mean something's wrong with you; you're a very loving person, but the other person doesn't see it through your eyes. When you fall for someone, you start to hope for a future together. You imagine dates and maybe even a relationship. But when you find out it's not going to happen, that's where it hurts. It can make you feel embarrassed, rejected, or even angry, especially if you've plucked up the courage to say how you feel. I can't put it any plainer than this: relationships are complicated, full stop. Rejection can be one of the most challenging aspects of being a teenager. You might have spent weeks or even months rehearsing what to say, practising your words, or waiting for the right moment. When the moment finally comes and they say no, or worse, don't respond the way you hoped, it can feel crushing. It's important to remind yourself that being brave enough to express your feelings is something to be proud of, no matter the outcome. Rejection doesn't mean you're not good enough. It simply means that the other person doesn't feel the same way, and this is something you can't control. What you can control is how you handle it, but I understand that this is easier said than done.

It's not just sadness that they did this to you, but it can feel like real pain, like it's the end of the world. You might start wondering if you're not good enough. You might ask yourself, "What's wrong with me?" But the truth is, there's nothing wrong with you at all. Please be kind to yourself; it may feel embarrassing and hurtful, but you've done a very brave thing. It might feel worse if they respond by saying they just want to be friends, but the damage has already been done, and this is a very tough one to deal with, especially when you have to push down your feelings because they just want to be friends.

This can make you feel invisible. You might see them talking to someone else and feel a sharp sting in your chest. You might also start comparing yourself to the people they're talking to, wondering why you can't be like them: funnier, cooler, or better-looking. If you were, they'd like you. But my dear friend, love doesn't work like that. It's not about being perfect. It's about connection. And if that connection isn't there, it's not your fault. It doesn't mean you're any less special. Please don't try harder, hoping that they'll change their mind.

You are wonderful,
You are beautiful,
You are more than enough.

It's not about dressing differently, acting differently, or saying the perfect thing so they'll finally notice you. This false idea is everywhere in movies, on social media, and in books. But truthfully, in real life, love doesn't work like that. Thinking like this can be very dangerous. It makes you forget your own value. You might spend too much time thinking about this person and not enough time thinking about yourself. By doing this, you might ignore people who do like you, see you, and want you to notice them, but because you're so focused on the one who doesn't, you fail to open your eyes and glance around. It's not fair to you. It's okay to feel sad. But don't let yourself believe that you have to earn someone's love.

So, how do you get through it? First, know that it's okay to be upset. You don't have to pretend it doesn't hurt, and don't tell yourself you're being dramatic. You're allowed to cry, but you need to protect your beautiful heart and learn from what you're experiencing. Accepting your feelings is the first step to healing. If you're always around the person you love, it's hard to move on, especially when they may have rejected your love or brushed it off as you being silly. Please try to take a step back, and if you can, spend less time with them or even unfollow them on social media for a while. It's not being mean; it's self-care. You need to give your heart a little space to heal.

I know you might feel embarrassed to tell your friends… they might have seen the way you reacted anyway, hurt and confused, but now that it's in the open, you can talk about it, which is okay. You did a brave thing, so be proud of yourself for finally letting it out. It's their choice, and you deserve to look after yourself. Talk to your friends about what happened, but don't let hate get in the way of your thinking, because they rejected you. Remember, it's part of growing up. Try talking to someone else you trust, such as a family member, teacher, or school counsellor. One thing to understand here is that everyone has been through rejection and unrequited love. It's how we all learn to find meaningful relationships and what works, and what doesn't. Please don't keep your feelings bottled up; it won't make the situation any better. Talking about your feelings and listening to others share their experiences helps your heart soften to the pain.

If the person is in your class, unrequited love can feel even more overwhelming. The constant reminder can make it harder to move on. If you have to work on a group project with them or share the same friends, the situation can feel like a never-ending spiral of hurt. This is where you try to set some boundaries to protect your emotions. Perhaps you could quietly ask a teacher to place you in a different group or seat farther away from them. Hopefully, in your school, most teachers should understand what you're going through and give you a pretend punishment, which will make the seating change a little less conspicuous, rather than move you to another place. These changes may seem small, but they can help create some breathing room in the moment.

The school environment can also be a place where healing happens. You could join a new club, discover a subject you love, or meet someone new who shares your interests. Use this time to grow, not just in your subjects but personally. Please remember, this isn't about distracting your mind while your heart is still holding onto the hope that things will change between the two of you. If they do… only time will bring you together, as you both mature into young adults, feelings change, and so does life. But don't do this to yourself; you deserve better, and waiting isn't helping you to develop or be kind to yourself.

Try something you've never done before, like stepping out of your comfort zone with drama, a sports team, or volunteering for something. By doing so, you help connect with different people and build your confidence. And who knows? You might find someone new who appreciates you for exactly who you are.

There are also things you should avoid doing. Don't check their social media every day, hoping for a clue that they like you back. Please don't send them texts trying to stay close. Don't try to make them jealous. Don't blame them or try to change yourself... for them. And most importantly, don't give up on finding your heart completely. If you're beginning to bottle things up, feel very sad (for a long time), or if you start having trouble eating, sleeping, or focusing at school, you need to talk to someone.

*Don't chase after someone who
doesn't feel the same as you.
You deserve more.*

12. Hate in the Mirror
Understanding and Overcoming Self-Hatred

Self-hatred is more than just feeling bad about yourself. It's a deep, painful belief that you're never good enough, that something is wrong with you, or that you don't deserve kindness or happiness. This feeling can sneak up on anyone, but it generally comes from long-term abuse of always being put down, especially when dealing with family issues, bullying, being rejected, or struggling with your own identity in your surroundings or culture. For teenagers, it's common to be hard on yourself. But when that voice in your head becomes cruel or constant, it can take over your life. And it's not only this; what if the voices are just echoes of your parents' hurtful words going around and around until you start to believe them? Your inner critic is always whispering that you're a failure, a burden, or unlovable. It can make you second-guess everything, from how you look, to how you speak, to whether people actually care about you. It can tell you that your mistakes are proof that you're worthless. It can also turn the silence of others into the reason you believe you're being judged or forgotten.

What's worse is that self-hatred is quiet. It doesn't shout. It just sits inside, growing, especially when you don't talk about it. Sometimes it shows up in how you treat yourself. Maybe to the extent that you start avoiding mirrors. Maybe you stop trying because you assume you'll fail. Maybe you begin hurting yourself, physically or emotionally, because you believe… you deserve the pain. These feelings are real, but they are not facts. They're not your fault. And most importantly, they can be challenged.

Self-hatred often begins when painful things happen that are out of your control. You might be growing up in a family where you feel invisible or unloved. It may be a result of being bullied at school or online. You might also compare yourself to people, whether in real life or on social media, who seem perfect. Sometimes it grows to the point where you feel you can never be 'enough'.

You're not smart enough.
You're not attractive enough.
You're not liked enough.

The brutal truth is, the world can be a very harsh place. It shouldn't be, but it is, and if no one helps you make sense of the pain, you might start blaming yourself for all of it.

You aren't born hating yourself. These feelings are learnt over time, and because they were learnt, they can also be unlearnt. Learning to deal with self-hatred isn't about ignoring your pain. It's about learning to see yourself in a better light over time. It means separating the reality from the lies. It's true that you can't please everyone, but just because people say hurtful things to you, doesn't make them true. So, please stop believing everything you hear, just like on the internet, don't believe everything you see or read… it's just the same for you. You might be used to saying things to yourself, "I'm just being honest with myself," when really, you're being unfair and unkind to yourself.

Being honest doesn't mean tearing yourself apart. True honesty involves acknowledging your strengths, weaknesses, struggles, and areas of growth. You're a teenager, you're not perfect, and neither is anyone around you. It's our flaws and weaknesses that make us unique. You are what you believe you are! Say it,

I am beautiful,
I am smart,
I am creative as anyone else in this world.

You deserve to be loved and deserve to love yourself. What are you beating yourself up over? When broken down to the tiny elements, it turns out to be nothing more than your own creation of someone else's hurtful words. Hurtful people bully anyone around them, but it still doesn't make anything they do or say, stick.

You deserve better than a life spent attacking yourself. Even if you've messed up, even if you don't always love who you are, you still deserve to be kind to yourself.

Your world matters.
Your heart matters.
You matter.

The validity of your emotions is how you manifest them in your mind. Now, you asked yourself… but what can I do? I hate everything about myself.

Let's start by understanding where these feelings come from, how to talk back to them, and how to rebuild a relationship with yourself.

What if I told you that we all have that voice in our head, throwing sarcasm, hurtful regret, and yes, hatred, too, at us? The face in the mirror, the eyes from the corner of the dark screen, the reflection in your cup, always there staring, scowling, or frowning. You think you're alone, sorry… but you're in a club, no membership fees, and you didn't sign a contract to join. There is no quick fix to eliminate it, but there is a way forward. And it begins with you choosing to believe that you're worth fighting for.

You might have started to hate yourself over a long period, with little things you didn't like, how you did them, or what you said, or they might come from one intense moment that changed how you see yourself. Either way, what causes these feelings is often outside your control, especially when you're still a teenager and developing an identity of who you are.

The negativity you have towards yourself may come from your own home. Perhaps you've been growing up hearing hurtful things from your parents, brothers, or sisters. "You're too much, too loud, too sensitive, or never good enough." Maybe your family expects perfection, and any mistake makes you feel like a disappointment. When your family is supposed to love you most and treats you like a problem, it's easy to start believing they're right. Even if they didn't mean to hurt you, their words or actions might leave scars that never heal. Other times, the world outside becomes the source. Being bullied at school or online can damage your self-image when you get side-swiped by one brutal comment that you didn't see coming. Hurtful words, teasing, or rejection can make you feel like you're always the wrong shape, wrong colour, wrong size, wrong everything. This constant pressure can lead you to believe that you're never good enough. Now, think about the comments, even if you were perfect, ask yourself: do you think their comments would be any different? I think you know the answer to this is… probably, no!

It could manifest from 'trauma' in some form. Aeona had her scars on show for all to see. When people saw her, they felt pity for the pain, thinking how horrible it must have been to be burnt like that, but in Aeona's eyes, she felt that they knew she was the cause of the burns. A label of judgement, blame, like she deserved it. She hated herself to the core, swearing never to look in the mirror again and on top of this, in the way her mother treated her. If you've experienced things like abuse, neglect, or abandonment, it can lead to deep emotional wounds. These may often turn inward. You might start thinking you were to blame, even when you weren't. It becomes easier to hate yourself than to face how unfair or painful the situation really is. However, blaming yourself for being hurt is not the answer; it perpetuates the hurt.

Social media plays a huge role. It shows you images of what your life is "supposed" to look like: perfect bodies, flawless skin, smiling families, and amazing friendships. But most of what you see online is filtered and edited. Comparing yourself to the impossible version of 'Expected False Reality' can make your 'Real-Self' feel like it falls short. Over time, this chipping away at your confidence leaves you feeling ashamed of who you are.

Self-hatred may have started with someone else's actions or society's messages, but healing begins with you. You're not broken. You're carrying pain that was never meant to be yours. You can learn to set it down, one piece at a time.

All possible causes are discussed throughout this book, in various sections, and all focus on the hatred of you. So, what do you expect? The words hurt. My heart hurts just thinking about what you're going through. Every section brings tears, pain, and talks about quietly suffering alone, but here is where you make a stand. You are strong, this is about you, my friend. HERE you are loved, HERE you are heard, and HERE you are seen.

These words are just as powerful as any hurtful stare you get back from the mirror, but when expressed through kindness, care and love for yourself, they become even more powerful.

How do I handle this?

One of the first signs is negative self-talk. You might start to think things like, "I'm so stupid," "I mess up everything," or "No one really likes me." These thoughts can pop up during stressful moments or even when everything seems fine. Over time, they can start to feel normal, even though they're not fair or true. If you're hearing these kinds of thoughts often, it's a signal that your inner voice has turned against you.

"I'm stupid, I messed up," is not the same as, "I messed up, I feel stupid."

In the first one, you're already putting yourself down; you're placing your intelligence at the forefront. In the second, the focus is on you 'messing up.' We all make mistakes; it's a learning process. If we got everything right the first time, how would we learn anything? Why not try saying, "I messed up, I need to practise more," or, "I messed up, how can I do it differently next time?" It doesn't matter what you did, but your response to it does. It's the same if someone else makes the comments: "You're so stupid, you messed up!" Your response could be, "Yes, you're right, I messed up, let me see how I can fix it." Maybe you can, maybe you can't. Either way, it isn't a reflection of all of you, just on a particular task or a particular time.

Another way self-hatred shows up is when you start pulling away from people. You might stop texting back, avoid hanging out, or pretend everything's fine just so no one asks questions. Being around others might also feel exhausting or scary because you're afraid they'll see the parts of you that you're trying to hide. (Self-harm is discussed later). You may start keeping secrets, not because you want to lie, but because you feel ashamed or believe you don't deserve their support. It can get to the point where you no longer care about anything: your hygiene, skipping meals, sleeping too much, or barely sleeping at all. You might wear clothes that hide your body, or cuts and other marks, or avoid mirrors altogether. These behaviours are often a way of coping with discomfort or shame, even if you don't fully realise it at the time.

How many times have you made yourself invisible? You've mastered the art of it to the extent that the teacher probably never calls out your name. You avoid raising your hand in class, stop speaking out when something bothers you, or never cause problems. Some people struggle with self-hatred by trying to prove their worth by pushing themselves too hard. This could mean taking on every task, always aiming for perfection, or saying yes to things just to be liked. Both extremes come from the same place: the fear that you aren't enough as you are. Remember, you should do things for yourself, not to meet someone else's expectations. You might not immediately connect the above actions to self-hatred, as most seem like normal reactions to stress, sadness, or life's challenges. However, when they persist for a long time and start to impact your daily feelings, it's time to look more closely. Recognising these patterns isn't about blaming yourself. It's about giving yourself a chance to understand what you're feeling and why.

Starting to Heal

Healing from self-hatred doesn't mean waking up one day and suddenly loving everything about yourself. It begins with small changes, like treating yourself with more patience and less harshness. Everything might feel awkward or even fake at first, but they're part of building a better relationship with yourself.

"How do I stop this voice in my head?"

Look at it like you're your own best friend. If you wouldn't say the exact words to a friend, then the words aren't worth listening to. Replacing hurtful words with more understanding ones might sound simple, but it takes time and practice. The voice will win a lot of the time, but with patience and practice, you'll be able to put words into its mouth, so to speak.

'Why are you doing it like that, stupid?'

'A good try, I'm sure you can do it better next time.'

These kinds of statements can interrupt the cycle of self-criticism and help build a more supportive inner voice and mindset.

You've read this so many times in the previous sections, you know the drill. Back to talking to someone you trust. Not every adult is a trusted person with this topic, especially in the next section. Please find someone who listens to you. It goes without saying… without judgement. Saying things out loud makes them real, but it also gives others the chance to remind you of the parts of yourself you've forgotten. The great parts can be overshadowed by the negativity of your inner voice and of those hurtful people around you. Everyone needs help sometimes; you don't have to carry the pain alone.

Writing, drawing, painting, or playing music are forms of creative expression that can also be powerful tools. They allow you to let out thoughts and feelings. You don't need to be "good" at them; the point isn't perfection. Nothing is ever about being perfect. A lot of our negative reflection stems from aiming our goals too high. You can do this if you want to be an Olympic athlete, an artist, or pursue another goal, but even then, to reach the top, it's a step-by-step process that can take years to perfect. What we're talking about is release. The more you let these feelings out, the less power they have inside you.

While we're discussing sports, taking care of your body can also benefit your mind. Sleep, movement, hydration, and eating regular meals are small actions that tell your brain you matter. When you treat yourself with basic care, even when you don't feel like it, you start to rebuild the belief that you're worth taking care of. These habits don't erase pain, but they create a steady ground to stand on while you work through it. It also helps if you learn how to acknowledge and accept your emotions instead of fighting them. Feelings like sadness, anger, or shame aren't dangerous. They are signals, not signs of weakness. Try naming them without judgment: "I feel lonely right now," or "I'm feeling overwhelmed." This practice of noticing instead of reacting gives you space to respond with kindness instead of punishment.

If you like writing or expressing yourself on paper, you might find strength in keeping a journal or happiness lists. Write down what you did in the day, paying attention to how you were feeling and what the task was at the time. Taking note of the different emotions can help you to be positive and gain strength over your inner voice. If you enjoy talking, you could try therapy sessions, join peer support groups, or set goals to reduce self-critical thoughts each week. There's no single path to healing, but every path begins with believing that you can do it.

By making slow, subtle changes, you don't have to stay stuck in a place of self-hate. It's okay to take your time; it's about finding peace inside, not about your outward appearance, because you are a beautiful person. The truth is, you're not the cruel things you've told yourself. You're a person with value, with strength, and with a future that doesn't have to look like your past. Every small step toward kindness is a step toward freedom. And every time you choose to try again, even when it's hard, you're choosing to believe in your worth.

Even after you begin to heal, there will be days when self-hatred tries to pull you down. You might think you've made progress, and then one tough moment brings all the old feelings rushing back. That doesn't mean you've failed. It means you're having a slip. It isn't a straight path. It curves, it dips, and sometimes it circles back. On hard days, remind yourself of the tools you've learned. Revisit your journal, your support network, or the habits that help you feel steady. Allow yourself to feel what you feel without getting lost in it. On some days, your goal might be to just get through the day. That's still a victory.

When self-hatred shows up again, don't fight it with more hate. You won't feel better by yelling at yourself to "just stop feeling this way." Instead, get curious. Ask, "Where is this coming from today?" Maybe it's a tough conversation you're going to have with yourself, but it's going to be okay.

13. Understanding Food
Looking in the mirror

We all need food; that's a fact you must agree with. But sometimes our brains confuse us into thinking differently. Sometimes it tells us we don't need it, or we need to keep eating continuously. If you feel like this, it's okay to some extent, but when it gets out of hand, that's when you need to sit back and think about what's happening, because it can become quite dangerous. You may not want to hear it, or tell yourself you're doing this for a purpose, which is again… fine, but if you wake up every morning and the first thing you do is jump on the scales, you may need to reset your routines. Focusing on every little change or micro-fluctuation in your weight isn't a healthy way to gauge whether you're gaining, losing, or changing body shape. This is how most eating disorders start.

To understand where you are, let's look at several factors that may be contributing to your situation.

Being self-conscious

If you're a teenager reading this, it's not unusual for you to start thinking about your body and how you look, especially as your body is changing the most right now. You're more aware of how others perceive you, and scrolling through social media, which is full of images of people showcasing what a "perfect" body should look like, doesn't help. It's easy to look in the mirror and wish you looked like them. You're no different from millions of other people doing exactly what you're doing: setting yourself expectations. Sometimes, we seem to set them far too high, and that's where problems can arise.

Perhaps you look in the mirror every morning and pull your clothes tight to see how your stomach looks, or step on the scales to check if you've gained weight. It's okay to want to lose weight, build more muscle, achieve a six-pack, or feel more confident. This pushes most teenagers towards dieting. However, it's crucial to understand what dieting entails and whether it's a healthy approach or not.

First, let's discuss what your body is doing right now. You're growing... a lot. Your bones are getting longer, your muscles are developing, and your brain is changing, too. Depending on how fast everything is growing, you might even feel strange pains in your body, but you can't quite put a finger on where exactly they're coming from. It takes an enormous amount of energy and nutrients to sustain this growth spurt. This is why your body needs food, not just for the enjoyment or the taste, but for its essential needs to fuel your incredible body. If you start cutting out essential vitamins or skipping meals, you may miss out on the nutrients your body needs to build strength and stay healthy. This is why you need to consider and examine the facts before starting a diet. You're becoming a young adult, and your body is going to change no matter what you do. However, dieting may not be the best approach for you at this stage of your life. By all means, changing the way you eat, the amount, time, and types of food, is a good thing. However, without correct guidance, it may do more harm than good.

The reasons for wanting to diet may also be a deciding factor in whether you need to. Is it peer pressure to look a certain way? This can come from friends, family, celebrities, or influencers. You might have looked at images online of an 'ideal' body and begun to compare yourself to them, only to suddenly feel like you don't measure up or fall far short. But here's the truth: everyone's body is different. If it sounds like a cliché... it is. Some people are naturally thin, some have curves, and some are in between. There's no right way to look, and trying to change your body to match someone else's can lead to disappointment, self-isolation or worse. Some diets promise quick weight loss, but they often fail to deliver lasting results. Just think about it: you're going to work hard, cutting out so many things you like to eat, keeping yourself to a tight routine and cravings until you feel like you're going crazy. You'll lose weight at first, but then gain it back quickly at the sight of a burger, or you might even skip your 'free day' because you feel that you don't deserve it. Often, strict diets can leave you feeling tired, cranky, or make you more susceptible to illness. If you're not eating enough or skipping entire food groups, you're missing out on essential vitamins, minerals, and energy. This affects how you feel during the day, how well you focus at school, and even how your body develops.

So, how can you have a win-win? Well, just by adjusting the what, when and how you eat can have a profound effect on how you feel and definitely on how you look. Instead of dieting or extreme dieting (which we'll focus on later), focus on developing healthy eating habits. Eat a variety of foods: fruits, vegetables, whole grains, proteins, and healthy fats. An essential thing is to drink plenty of water. Moving your body… You may not like going to the gym or feel embarrassed, depending on how self-conscious you are, but that's okay. Your feelings are valid, and you've done a great thing by wanting to make a change. You want to be more toned, lean, and muscular. Whatever you do, you look great now, and you're going to look amazing with just a few subtle changes in your life. Whether it's walking, dancing, playing sports, or biking, any of these will help your body. Please don't give yourself a timeline. Yes, you want to look good, but if you've never exercised or reduced your food intake before, taking it easy at first is the best approach. This is supposed to be a fun change in your life.

If you're feeling unhappy with your body, talk to someone. Don't be shy; we've all looked in the mirror and thought, 'I don't like what I see!' Sometimes the problem isn't your body, it's how you're feeling about yourself. And that's something you can work on with kindness and help. As soon as you make it feel like a mission by overdoing it, the fun stops, and the pain begins. Then, you'll fall back and become frustrated with yourself and hopefully not. Still, you may move to the darker side of being body-conscious, as we move onto the following topics: Anorexia and Bulimia.

14. Binge and Purge
Understanding Bulimia Nervosa

So, why do some teenagers develop bulimia? It's a complicated question to start with. There's no one simple reason. It can come from a mix of things, like feeling pressure to look a certain way, being teased or bullied about your body, or struggling with anxiety, which can lead to depression. Movies or casual comments thrown at you from friends or family members can add to the pain of always looking your best... at all times.

In Chapter Thirty-one, police officer Rebecca had struggled all her life trying to maintain a recommended weight, but without help, she found it near enough impossible. All through her school life, she'd listened to hurtful comments from her peers and in the end even the teachers let the occasional comment slip out about her being overweight. It didn't seem to get any better being an adult either.

"Do me a favour, take a walk up the back lane to the monument. We have an individual fitting the description up there. Take Rebecca with you and check it out. Over."

She gave an affirmative and replaced the handset to the groans of her colleague in the back.

"Come on, Rebecca, you heard the man. Out you get, you lazy sod!"

"Why me? Take Evans with you. I don't like walking! That's why I came, to just sit in the car. It's what I do best," complained Rebecca. "Come on, take Evans! She likes walking. She's always talking about ho…"

"… and get into shit when he finds out, not a chance! Get the biscuits out of your face, and let's make a move!" she ordered, to the laughter of Evans beside her.

Rebecca didn't have any biscuits, but an implied comment or sniggering laugh, hurt all the same.

Another contributing factor that can push some individuals towards having an eating disorder is social media. Being pressurised, screen after screen, constantly hit with images of perfection, everywhere you turn, every new post. How can you compete with such expectations, other than by looking at yourself and thinking negatively?

How can you tell if something is real anymore?

Your emotions go into overload, and for many teenagers, the only way to cope with such pressure is to take drastic measures. However, my dear friend, it's important to know that having an eating disorder isn't a choice. It's not about vanity or you being dramatic, because all of the above cause real mental health trauma in a lot of teenagers. It's a form of emotional breakdown that needs real and immediate support. The myth that only girls go through this isn't true. Bulimia or BN can affect all teenagers. Anyone can feel trapped by pressure, body image, or anxiety.

Teenagers with bulimia often hide their behaviour. They may appear to eat normally in front of others, but binge when they're alone. You might notice someone who has wrappers in their bag, pockets, or stuffed under their pillow or clothes in the wardrobe, if you have a family member who's going through this. Sometimes, they become overly focused on their body, weighing themselves frequently or wearing baggy clothes to conceal changes. Please watch out for yourself, your family, and friends for some of the signs that they may be struggling. Another thing they might do is purge. They might eat in front of others to appear normal, but if you notice that they always go to the bathroom right after meals, or if you see signs of fatigue or mood changes, these could be red flags. After bingeing, the person might feel guilty or scared of gaining weight, so the only choice in their eyes is to get rid of the vital nutrients and vitamins they've just eaten, usually by making themselves sick.

Please watch for signs of hearing vomiting regularly, or being hit with the smell frequently. Continuous vomiting can often lead to throat, teeth or stomach damage. One more deceptive trick they may use is the use of laxatives. If you notice any wrappers in the bin or around, it can be a sign of the bulimia impulse. Using too many laxatives, especially when they're not needed, can progress to harming their internal organs, dehydration, heart problems, or even long-term health issues if not treated. This goes for you, too. Please look after yourself; you can't hide your pain for too long. Trying to compete with 'false standards' is a fruitless battle, which may lead to permanent damage to your body. I know it can make you feel ashamed, isolated, anxious, or depressed, but holding onto a heavy secret is a tough burden to carry. Life will be harder for you, and it doesn't have to be. You just don't realise how beautiful you are, inside and out. And if people put you down or say hurtful things, they don't deserve to be in the same room as you.

As you grow and go through school, you might start noticing changes not only in your body but also in how you feel about it. At first, someone with bulimia might look like they're just concerned about their weight. They might talk a lot about dieting, avoiding certain foods, or constantly trying to "eat clean." But underneath, there are deep emotional struggles like feeling not good enough, being scared of judgment, or trying to deal with stress or sadness. For many teens, bulimia becomes a way of trying to feel in control when everything else feels out of control.

Dealing with bulimia, whether it's yourself or someone you know, isn't an easy fix. The frequency of symptoms can range from mild to extreme, from one or two episodes per week to fifteen in extreme cases. You can show many signs leading to BN, but only a professional can actually diagnose whether you have it or not. They'll have to look at your history and behaviour leading up to it. Now, this is where you can either feel embarrassed about it or be in denial about having any issues. Sometimes, it may be difficult for you to come to terms with it. Please understand that you aren't bothering anyone and will never be a burden because of what you're going through. An early diagnosis is crucial so you can receive the best available treatment and support.

It may require a team of people who genuinely care about you. This might include a therapist, a nutritionist, and a doctor. Having a therapist has lost the stigma of the past, so there's no need to be embarrassed about anything. Everyone needs a little help sometimes, even you. They can help you get to the bottom of the stress, help you to understand your emotions, build your self-esteem, and teach you healthier ways to cope. A nutritionist can help you develop an understanding of your body and what it means to have a balanced diet. This will help if you feel you are a little overweight and will offer great ways to tone up and look great. They can also work with a doctor, who can conduct a physical health check-up to ensure you're safe and healing.

In some cases, support groups or teen recovery programmes can also help you connect with others who are experiencing the same challenges. You do realise that these people are here to give you the tools for you to get through this… without judgement or blame, because there's none to give. You're not broken, you're stressed out and need a little help.

Recovery from bulimia doesn't happen overnight. There will be setbacks and tough days, but with the right help, recovering from it is absolutely possible. You'll learn that your worth isn't tied to your appearance or your eating habits. You'll start to find joy in things outside of food or weight. Most of all, you'll begin to see yourself as someone who deserves care, kindness, and a full life. One helpful step is learning how to listen to your body again. When you've had bulimia, your hunger and fullness signals can get confused. You might not trust yourself to eat or stop eating. This is why it's essential to rebuild your relationship with food gradually, without feeling guilty or ashamed. Food isn't your enemy; it's fuel, and it's okay to enjoy eating.

It's also important to challenge those hurtful people around you… and that voice in your head telling you you're only valuable if you look a certain way. The voice can be so convincing, especially when you see idealised images online. Try shifting your focus to social media accounts that promote body positivity or real-life diversity. Spend time with people who support you, not judge you. Practise saying kind things to yourself, even if it feels weird at first. These small steps build confidence and can quiet the negative voice inside.

Please read through section: 'Hate in the Mirror' as it details other ways of having a positive outlook.

If you're supporting a friend who you think might have bulimia, approach them gently. Don't accuse or shame them. You could say something like, "I've noticed you don't seem like yourself lately, and I'm worried. If something's going on, I'm here to listen or help you find someone who can." Just knowing someone cares can be a big relief. Be patient. Your friend might not be ready to talk right away, but your support can still make a difference.

In the next section, we'll explore a more serious eating disorder: anorexia nervosa. Like bulimia, anorexia is more than just about food. It's about emotions, control, and self-worth. Understanding both of these disorders can help you recognise the signs, break the silence, and support yourself or a friend toward a healthier, kinder life.

15. Anorexia - a suffering disappearance

Anorexia nervosa, or AN, is more than just a desire to be thin. It's a complex mental health condition that affects millions of teenagers around the world. For many, it begins with a simple diet or a potentially hurtful comment that prompts a strong reaction. Over time, the desire to control your weight can become an obsession that takes over everything you do. It affects your physical health, relationships, self-esteem, and emotional wellbeing. You may be especially vulnerable due to the pressures of school, social media, and the developmental changes you're going through at this very important time in your life.

Before we examine AN in detail, I must share a harsh truth with you, and you need to understand this clearly from the outset. This isn't a game; time isn't on your side. You need to act now, as you're reading this and thinking it over. This section aims to offer you understanding, support, and practical steps to help you recognise that there's a dangerous problem within yourself or with someone you know. Whether you're struggling personally or worried about someone close to you, the most important thing to remember is that help is available and recovery is possible. I need you to do this, not for me, not for those around you, but for yourself.

Please reach out, not tomorrow, not the day after, but now!

Anorexia nervosa is an eating disorder characterised by extreme restriction of food intake, intense fear of gaining weight, and a distorted body image. People with it may see themselves as overweight even when they're dangerously underweight. They may go to great lengths to avoid eating, exercise excessively, or engage in ritualistic eating habits. Anorexia isn't just about food; it's deeply tied to emotions, self-worth, and control.

There are two main types of anorexia: the restricting type and the binge-eating/purging type, which we discussed in the previous section. Here, we're talking about the restrictive type, which involves extreme measures, such as weight loss through dieting, fasting, or excessive exercise. It's life-threatening if not treated. It can lead to serious medical complications such as heart problems, osteoporosis (a condition that weakens your bones and makes them fragile and susceptible to fractures, even from minor impacts like a fall or even something as small as a cough). It can also lead to kidney failure and even death due to the trauma it causes to your internal organs. But it's treatable, especially when caught early. This is why the emphasis is on the NOW, rather than later. Understanding the signs and symptoms is the first step in getting help. If you're questioning weight loss, avoiding meals, lying about eating, wearing baggy clothes, and are preoccupied with food, dieting, or body image, you need to take extra care that it isn't just a short phase you're going through, but something more sinister.

There's no single cause of anorexia. Instead, it's usually the result of a combination of factors. Studies have shown that it can run in families, meaning some people may be genetically susceptible to developing it. I know you may be embarrassed or feel that you might be shouted at, but you need to try to get to the bottom of it. Please bring the topic up quietly, if possible, with a family member or someone who might know. Perhaps you have a family member who's gone through or is currently going through a similar experience. Chemicals in your brain that control hunger, mood, and impulse may function differently in people with anorexia. Hormonal changes during puberty can also contribute to the development of eating disorders, so if you feel like blaming yourself and don't want anyone to know, here's the get-out clause: you can't get away from genetics. You'll at least eliminate this possibility just by quietly asking around.

Psychologically, anorexia is often linked to perfectionism, anxiety, low self-esteem, and a need for control. You might struggle with identity, emotional regulation, or past trauma and may use food restriction as a way to cope with overwhelming feelings.

Melanie, Aeona's aunt, went through a very difficult period when she was about fifteen. Her weight had dropped so dangerously low, she was admitted into hospital. Her heart rate was barely stable, and she was constantly cold and dizzy. For months, she'd been hiding meals, over-exercising, and withdrawing from friends and family. By the time she was taken to hospital, her condition was severe, both physically and mentally. Doctors said she was at risk of organ failure. She was placed on bed rest and monitored around the clock. At first, she resisted treatment because she didn't believe anything was wrong with her, and that she wasn't sick. This is quite a common thought among those with anorexia. But slowly, through medical care, nutritional support, and therapy, she began to understand what she was putting herself through. It wasn't just about food; it was about control, fear, and self-worth.

She had to stay in hospital for about six weeks. She wasn't fully recovered, but it was a vital turning point for her. The hospital gave her a safe place to begin healing, in both a physical and emotional sense. Over time, she began to see that accepting help wasn't a sign of weakness, it was strength. Recovery from anorexia is never linear, but Melanie's story shows that even in the darkest moments, there's a way forward.

Whatever you feel, your feelings are valid, and you may be hurting, shy, confused or overwhelmed. None of this is your fault; you're not to blame for any of the things that are swimming around your head. There are many ways to be kind to yourself… and this is never one of them. You may feel that social and cultural pressures play a significant role in what you're going through as well. In many societies, thinness is idealised and often equated with beauty, success, and worth. Social media amplifies these messages, exposing many teenagers, like yourself, to edited images and unhealthy body comparisons.

You're unique, special and worthy of so much more. Understanding the cause of any eating disorder involves looking at your own history, personality, and the environment you live in. Watch out for signs of intense anxiety, being very sad or upset, being irritable, or difficulty concentrating. All of these very upsetting things can lead to a lot of emotional concerns, not only for you, but for those around you.

While professional help is often necessary, there are also several steps you can take on your own to support and help yourself. Holding your hand up and acknowledging that you might be struggling to cope with some of the pressure and hardships around you is the first and bravest step to take. Living in denial or not wanting to admit you may have an issue is a powerful barrier to your own wellbeing. Please be honest with yourself; I know it might be tough, but it's the first act of courage in protecting your own heart and body. Writing down your thoughts and feelings about how you act around food, or what's going through your mind when you look in the mirror, can help you start to recognise patterns and triggers. I understand that you might not want to talk to someone… yet, but please find someone you trust. It could be a friend, parent, school counsellor, PE teacher or coach. You don't have to face this alone. Sharing your experience is scary, but it's a vital step towards not dying. I know it's hard, but you must reach out.

Next, limit your exposure to harmful influences, such as particular social media influencers who may not have your best interests in mind, which is also incredibly important. They're just after followers and spreading their ideology to others, some of whom don't even understand what they're doing in the first place. Everyone can now come up with an idea of how to look good, dress well, or lose weight, without thinking about the consequences. Please, my dear friend, when someone posts something, don't take it at face value;

always examine the evidence and step back to truly consider the person's intentions before acting.

Putting your finger in the fire because someone else does will probably get you a burnt finger.

Unfollow accounts that promote unhealthy body standards or trigger body comparisons or supposed healthy eating. Fill your feed with body-positive and recovery-focused content instead. Focus on what your body can do, rather than how it looks. Try activities that help you feel strong, calm, or expressive, such as yoga, dancing, painting, or writing. There are so many things that support getting into great shape, rather than some of the extreme measures that many people post online. Setting small, realistic goals, such as eating one extra snack per day, attending social events, or practising positive self-talk, can also guide you down the right path. And make sure you celebrate every step you take, because you deserve it.

I will be happy, look great, and receive the support and help I need. Leads to: I am happy with myself, I look great, I have excellent support, and I held my hand up.

You don't have to recover perfectly. You just have to keep going. And you don't have to do it alone. In the 'Resources' section at the back of this book, you can read more about this topic. Please reach out, be brave, call one of the helplines and talk about your worries. Please love who you are; even small changes can make a significant difference. By choosing to think, act, look or speak differently about yourself, a slight shift in one direction opens doors to opportunities you may not have seen before. Open your eyes to the love around you, and love will come back to you tenfold.

You matter, your heart matters. Look inside yourself; you're more than you think you're worth. You feel most people focus on the outside, but you'll be surprised to find that when you find love, they'll be more interested in your heart than what you see in the mirror.

16. Understanding Self-Harm

My dear friend, in the following two sections, we're going to discuss some painful topics and look at some of the truths behind them. So, I want you to be an adult for me, just for a little while.

Self-harm is a topic many of us struggle with, but few openly talk about. It causes confusion, it's frightening, and trying to understand it or come to terms with it is highly complex, especially if you're the one experiencing it. Self-harm, also called non-suicidal self-injury (NSSI), is the term used for someone who deliberately hurts their own body, usually as a way of coping with emotional pain, intense anger, and frustration. It's more common than you think, and it affects teenagers of all backgrounds, genders, and experiences.

Let's see if we can discuss it together, without judgment or shame. This is to help you understand what it is, why teenagers do it, and what healthier alternatives exist that may help. Whether you're struggling personally or worried about someone you care about, it's important to know that support is available and recovery is possible. Here, we have a safe space to learn, reflect, and take the first steps toward healing and dealing with a very distressing thing. Aeona is here, I am here, listening and guiding you at this difficult time. This is dedicated to you and those around you, with honesty, care, and respect for your experience of moving forward.

What Is Self-Harm?

Self-harm might include cutting, burning, hitting, scratching, or other forms of physical injury. While it can seem shocking to outsiders, for many who self-harm, it's a way to feel relief from emotional numbness, sadness, anger, or anxiety they're going through.

It's essential to understand that self-harm usually isn't about seeking attention or trying to end one's life. Instead, it's a coping mechanism, a way to deal with inner pain when words or other strategies feel unavailable. Some people feel a sense of release after hurting themselves, while others do it to punish themselves for something they've done or said, or because they have low self-esteem. The behaviour often becomes a cycle: similar to the addiction discussed previously, strong emotions build up, self-harm is used to release them, guilt or shame follows, and the emotions build again. Over time, this pattern becomes hard to break. Self-harm doesn't make problems go away, but it can feel like a temporary solution, which is why it's hard to stop.

The reasons behind it are complex and personal to you. There's no single cause, but several common factors often contribute. Emotional pain is usually at the centre of it; people may not know how to cope with difficult emotions or traumatic experiences, so they turn to physical pain as a distraction or release. These include depression, anxiety, overwhelming stress, or feelings of emptiness and numbness. Teenagers, like yourself, might use self-harm as a way to feel something when they feel disconnected from their emotions. It's sort of like an internal vs external response to… *why do I feel like this?* Or *why am I here?* Or you might use it to express anger or frustration that you can't show outwardly.

Psychological factors such as low self-worth, perfection- ism, or negative body image can also play a role, much like in *'Hate in the Mirror'* If you struggle with your identity, you're bullied, or feel misunderstood, you may be more vulnerable to act in particular ways, such as self-harm. Environmental influences like family conflict, neglect, abuse, or witnessing violence can also contribute to you hurting yourself. Other things, like academic and peer pressure or social media, can intensify feelings of inadequacy or failure. Perhaps you feel rejected, discriminated against, or experience a lack of acceptance, which can be a significant risk factor.

Aeona, through fear and as a release from her mum's rejection, did something… something small. She'd punch herself in the leg, a realisation of the sting; the pain didn't register. Yes, punching your own leg can be considered a form of self-harm, especially if it's done intentionally to cope with emotional pain, anger, numbness, or overwhelming thoughts. Self-harm isn't just about cutting or visible injuries. It includes any act where you deliberately hurt yourself (physically or emotionally) as a way of dealing with difficult emotions. This can also include hitting yourself, punching your leg, head, or arm, banging your head against something, or picking at an already scabbed wound. If you do any of this, it's still considered self-harm, whether anyone else can see it or not; a bruise is a bruise. Even if there are no visible injuries or blood, the act still counts and deserves compassion, and you need support.

It's pretty alarming to know that self-harm can also become a learned behaviour. If someone hears about it, sees it online, or knows a peer who self-harms, they may try it as a way to cope with their own struggles. It isn't about being weak or broken. It's a sign that someone is in pain and needs healthier tools to cope.

How It Affects You.

Self-harm might offer temporary relief, but it carries serious, possibly long-term, emotional, physical, and social consequences. Physically, injuries can lead to infections, scarring, and accidental harm that's more severe than intended. Over time, the body may not heal as easily, and the risk of permanent damage increases. Emotionally, self-harm often leads to feelings of guilt, shame, and isolation. You might start to hide your injuries, if not already, or withdraw from relationships. The secrecy can make you feel alone, even when you're surrounded by others. The more isolated you feel, the harder it becomes to reach out for help. It's a vicious circle if not checked.

The worst thing about self-harm is the mental trauma, as it can reinforce negative thought patterns about everything we do. You may begin to believe you deserve pain or that you can't cope without it. You can never find the answer in doing it; the escape is only short-lived. Please don't put yourself through it, my friend. Aeona understood what she was doing and she stopped early, so can you. You deserve to feel love, not pain, and if you can't find it at the moment, please continue reading and try some of the recommendations in this book. If not addressed, these thoughts can become deeply ingrained and increase the risk of depression or suicidal ideation. The more self-harm becomes a go-to coping mechanism, the harder it is for you to imagine life without it.

In a broader picture, socially, self-harm can put a real strain on relationships, because friends may not understand the what or the whys behind your actions.

Here, you need to stop and think.

Suppose they found out by accident, as you've been keeping the marks hidden. It's okay that they know. This is where healing is going to start to take place. It isn't yours to own by yourself any more. They might react with fear or anger, and the trust you had may erode somewhat. You may find it challenging to participate in activities where your injuries are visible, leading to avoidance and isolation. Now that it's out in the open, you may still hide the marks, but they can now be discussed little by little, reason by reason, and emotion by emotion.

Ultimately, self-harm doesn't solve the underlying problems, it only masks the hurt temporarily. But acknowledging its impact and opening up is an important step toward healing and finding new ways to cope.

17. Self-Help
What to do?

Taking steps to help yourself is one of the bravest and most important choices you can make. Even if you're not ready to talk to someone yet, there are ways to start shifting your relationship with self-harm. First, try to identify what emotions or situations trigger the urge to harm. Is it after arguments, when you feel rejected, or when anxiety builds up? Writing in a diary can help you trace these patterns, if you're emotionally ready. If you feel you aren't ready to open up, even to yourself, please try to take a deep breath and look at the situation from a different perspective, as if you were sitting to one side, watching yourself. Imagine the way you're sitting, feeling, fidgeting... can you see anything forming into a picture of the situation? Maybe you can find some clarity or a trend forming in your mind. Breathe in through your nose and out through your mouth. What you may be feeling is something akin to a panic attack, and this may be the point which triggers your outflow of emotions, which manifests as self-harm.

Next, create a list of alternative coping strategies tailored to different needs. For example, if you need a physical outlet, try squeezing an ice cube. Get an ice cube and, with all of your strength, try to break it. The chances are slim, but you feel the hardness of the object in your hand. The heat of your frustration melting the ice… the coldness seeping through your fingers. The transition from one form to another is like your heart: the love you have for yourself softens, quiets, and releases.

I feel you, my friend. Let it go. I know this is the start of a new awakening. If you still feel the urge to release your pain, frustration and anger, a safer escape is snapping a rubber band on your wrist.

One step at a time.

The rubber band is a safer way to release your distress. I know you're hurting, but we need a different mental and physical distraction to block out the hurt. Try intense exercise, drawing the emotion on paper (screw it up and throw it at the wall), or screaming into a pillow. Please try anything to let out the rage. The pain will pass, and the hurt will stop.

If you're feeling numb, take a cold shower (not hot). If the urge comes on all of a sudden, stand in the shower with your clothes on and turn on the cold tap. The blast of cold water will shock your body back to reality. I'm not sugar-coating this; we've come too far together to soften the brutal truth now.

I don't know if you listen to music or what your interests are, but if you do, try varying the genre you usually listen to. By doing this, you might find that your emotions shift in one direction or another. Experimenting with sound can also help you discover specific beats, singers, or rhythms that alter your thinking, personality, and even your posture. If you feel your chest tightening with a fast beat, slow it down or completely switch to 'classical' or 'dance.' Heavy rock may trigger episodes of rage or anger, but rap doesn't, or vice versa. Nyxa listened to a lot of heavy metal, mostly to drown out memories of hurt. But she also, at times, forced herself to breathe in deeply through her nose and out of her mouth while counting down from ten. She would calm herself by listening to sounds of nature, like a quiet stream trickling over rocks, with birds gently singing in the forest. Other times, she would search for 'rain and distant thunder sounds.' Please find what works for you. If you ever feel like trying to listen to forest sounds or rain, you'll find QR codes at the back of this book, allowing you to access them easily.

In addition to music, you might have gathered a few items that remind you of happy times. A memory-box containing a special scent of a perfume, a flower, images, whatever memory that brings a tear to the corner of your eye. Reflect on the fond memories you have with the object, focusing mainly on the event and the love you felt at that time. Place it in your box so you can retrieve it every time you need to reset. You could also include some handwritten notes, reminding you of your strengths and the reasons you deserve to be loved. Keeping these close by can help soften the blow when urges to release pain come unexpectedly.

Something that helps everyone is having a structured routine. It can reduce the feeling of vulnerability, so aim to maintain regular sleep patterns and meal timings. Establishing a schedule provides structure to your body clock, and after a week or so, your brain and the rollercoaster of emotions will become more integrated into your system. When you think of it, our bodies are generally made up of water, so it only makes sense to also drink a lot. I'm not talking about you *must* drink X amount, because you and I know it's too difficult to hit the mark.

Please avoid overloading your schedule, as the pressure of taking on so much can increase anxiety and hopelessness when things become out of control and we can't push back. At the other end of the scale is withdrawing or isolating yourself from others. It's okay to have alone time, but remember the voice in your head is the most active in these times. Later on, you can increase the amount of alone time you have, but it's best to keep these short for the time being.

As discussed earlier about the possibility that self-harm is a learnt trait, try to stay clear of environments or content that might reinforce urges, including some chat forums or social media pages that normalise or romanticise self-harm. There are many wonderful social media sites and posts that promote wellbeing, rather than put you down, discuss negative things, and generally use hate, irrelevant, or offensive content to provoke a reaction in online discussions. Be honest with yourself, do you really need to expose yourself to it all? You will begin to love yourself. It may be that you seem a little distracted at the moment, but you're going to change your outlook to be a more positive, self-caring teenager. Surround yourself with voices and social media that focus on growth and happiness.

Celebrate even the smallest thing you do, the effort you make to resist self-harm. If you go a day, a few hours, or even five minutes longer than usual without acting on an urge, that's real progress. I am so proud of you for trying to move forward. You can also keep a visual tracker, such as a calendar or a jar of beads. Drop a new bead in the jar every time you smile, every time you care for yourself and every time you sit on your hands instead of hurting yourself. Each bead represents a small win. See how many you can put in the jar. If fewer beads go in one day and more beads go in the rest, it's okay. One win is more than enough. You need love, you deserve love, and you will love. Let each one serve as a reminder that change is possible.

Lastly, allow yourself to feel proud of wanting to mend your heart, which was once whole. You may not have all the answers yet, but the fact that you're looking for ways to cope shows strength. Recovery doesn't happen in isolation, and you deserve support along the way.

18. When to Get Professional Help

Now, we need to talk more seriously as we're moving to the next level of self-harm. If you've tried all the self-help strategies and they don't seem to be working, nor does the help from your friends, you might have to ask for professional help. If you or someone you care about feels trapped in a cycle of self-harm, or if injuries are becoming more severe or frequent, it's essential to involve professionals.

It's especially important if your self-harming increases because of depression, anxiety, trauma, or suicidal thoughts. (We will sadly talk about the latter in the next section.) Mental health providers are trained to identify possible underlying causes and may be able to teach you new skills not listed here. They'll help you cope with distress, plan for regulating your emotions, and help rebuild your self-esteem. They might also introduce you to DBT (Dialectical Behaviour Therapy), which is specifically designed to help teenagers with intense emotions or self-destructive behaviour. Another term is CBT (Cognitive Behavioural Therapy), which can also help reframe harmful patterns and build coping mechanisms to lessen the hurtful thoughts.

It's okay to feel nervous or unsure when seeking professional help. The first appointment may involve discussing what's been going on with you and what kind of support you're looking for. You don't have to share everything at once. You're in control, and it's about you, and no one else. If you choose to go down this route, I'm very proud of you for putting yourself outside your comfort zone. Well done! It means you're choosing to prioritise your health and wellbeing. Think of it like seeing a doctor for an emotional wound, because your heart deserves care, too.

'Recovery from self-harm' isn't a term I'd use, because you're not recovering from anything; you're not broken, you're just a little scared of how intense emotions can be. It's a rediscovery of who you can be and how powerful you are. It may feel daunting to reach out, but you are strong. It doesn't mean you'll never struggle again, but it means you've begun to face emotional storms without turning to harm. If you relapse, it happens; don't give up. It's not failure; it's a sign that more support or a different strategy is needed. Return to your tools, reconnect with your reasons and reach out for help. You're learning, growing, and becoming stronger each time. Please remember, you're far from alone. Many others have walked your path and come out stronger, become more self-aware, and most of all, learnt to be more compassionate and self-loving.

19. Self-Destruction
The voice in your head

If you're here reading this and you've already started looking into ways to end your life, I need you to hear something before anything else: I'm so sorry that you're feeling this way. I'm so sorry life has become this heavy, this painful, this hopeless. And I want you to know, you aren't alone.

Even if it feels like no one sees you or understands what you're going through, there are people who care, people who want you to survive, and people who can help. You might not like the people around you, or they may have said hurtful words, but stay here with me and let's get through this. You being here, reading these words, still breathing through this moment, matters more than you might realise. It means that somewhere, deep down, even if you can't feel it clearly, a part of you still wants something to change. A part of you still wants help. That part of you deserves to be protected, listened to, and nurtured.

When someone starts searching for specific ways to leave this world, it usually means that the pain they're carrying has reached a point where it feels unbearable. Maybe you've tried to talk to people in your life, and they didn't get it. Maybe they brushed you off, told you to be strong and toughen up, or that you were being too dramatic or inconvenient. Or maybe you haven't told anyone because you're afraid… afraid of being judged, locked away, misunderstood, or seen as broken. This fear makes sense to me because I hear you. So many people are taught to suffer in silence, to push through without showing how badly they're hurting. But the truth is, suffering in silence doesn't make you stronger. It just makes you feel more alone. And you don't have to do this by yourself. Not now. Not ever.

Suicidal thoughts aren't really about wanting to die; they're about not knowing how to keep living like this. They're about you feeling overwhelmed, exhausted, hopeless, or invisible. They often come from a place of deep emotional pain that feels like it has no end. When you're in that space, your brain starts scanning for escape routes. This isn't weakness. This is your mind trying to protect you, the only way it knows how. However, the problem is that these thoughts are deceiving you. That voice in your head is telling you that nothing will ever get better, you're a burden, and that no one would care if you were gone.

The voice sounds like you, it mimics you… it's so convincing, but the facts are incorrect. The voice is just a symptom, just like any physical pain; your body is injured, and these thoughts are when your emotional pain has hit its limit.

A thought is all it should be, my friend:
nothing more and nothing less, just a thought.

It's okay to feel what you're feeling. It's okay to admit that you're not okay. You don't have to put on a brave face or pretend everything's fine when it isn't. You don't have to be "fixed" to be worthy of love, support, or life, because honestly, you're not broken, anyway. You have to be honest with yourself and with others. That honesty can be the first step out of the darkness. You don't need to have perfect words. You can say, "I'm not okay," or "I've been thinking about hurting myself," or even, "I don't want to feel like this anymore." That's enough. That's brave. And that's the kind of truth that can make you wake up feeling a little better.

You might be thinking, "But I've already tried asking for help. Nothing changed." Or maybe someone made you feel worse, like your pain wasn't serious or that you should "get over it." If that happened, I want you to know: they were wrong. Your pain is real. It deserves to be taken seriously. And just because one person didn't respond with care, doesn't mean no one ever will. There are people out there who will listen. It might be a counsellor, a therapist, or a teacher. Reach out to anyone you trust. There are many people like you. Please believe that you're not alone, and you're not the only one. Hang on in there. People who understand what it's like to feel broken inside, and who know how to help you begin the slow process of putting the pieces back together.

Sometimes, people hold off asking for help, and you're no different, maybe because you're afraid you'll be hospitalised or lose control over your life. This fear is valid. But asking for help doesn't automatically mean you'll be placed in a safe place where trained people can look after you and give you the best help they think you need. Mental health professionals are trained to support you while making sure you keep your independence in meeting your needs. The doctors' and specialists' goals aren't to take control away from you, but to give you the help so you can feel safe again, in your own skin, in your own life. If you ever reach a point where you're not safe, then yes, they will provide you with more urgent care. It may feel like a form of punishment, but please remember that if it comes to this point, you deserve protection, even tough love, although it may feel extremely harsh.

If the thoughts you're having are specific and persistent, and you've started making plans or exploring methods, then it's especially important to pause, now. It's never too late, even if you feel you've already made up your mind. But the truth is, you're still here, still reading, still breathing. Your story doesn't end this way. This is what you're in right now: the start of a new beginning. Just as Aeona found direction, began a new chapter in her life, and went down a different fork in her story… I have been truthful with you throughout this guide because you deserve the truth. We've been through many hurtful topics and have experienced a lot of pain together. But here, we have to stop for a minute. I created Aeona in the story and put her character through so much emotional pain. I did this for a purpose, and that was so you, through her suffering, would see a light. Her story is one of reflection to guide you, to help you, and to provide you with some tools to navigate difficult times. This is why you will reach out to someone, and in a little while, you will look back on this paragraph as the moment when things began to change. You don't have to believe in that yet. You just have to stay alive long enough to see if it could be true.

There are specific things you can do, even at this very moment, to make it through when it feels like too much. First, get physically safe. Remove anything around you that could be used to hurt yourself. If you can, tell someone nearby that you're not okay. If that's too hard, send a text or write a note. If you're alone and afraid you might act on your thoughts, please reach out to any one of the crisis lines at the back of this book. If you think you're in immediate danger, call emergency services or go to the nearest hospital. You're worth more than anything in the world, you're worth protecting, and your life matters too much to gamble with.

Even if you're not in immediate crisis or danger, but you're still thinking a lot about ending it all, you can begin building a personal safety plan. This includes identifying triggers. It might be a person, a location, an image, or something completely different. Please make a list of all the good things to stay for: even if it's just one small thing. What about a pet, a sibling, a moment or something you want to see? A bucket list can be of great help. There is so much to see and do, you can go anywhere and do anything. At the moment, things may seem impossible due to money, or you may think, 'I'm only a teenager.' But having goals is something to strive for. Start small… how about learning a new skill? What about adding going to the Pyramids, the Great Barrier Reef, or even running a marathon?

A bucket list gives you meaning, focus, and direction. Keep your plan in a safe location, such as on your phone or in a written format. It's not a magic fix, but it's a way to remind yourself that you have choices. These can get you through the next hour, and the one after that and so on.

Grounding yourself in the present can also help interrupt the intensity of your thoughts and that persistent voice. You can try holding something cold, an ice cube, or splashing your face with cold water. Focus on your senses: what you can see, hear, feel, smell, and taste. If one of them is overwhelming, please block it out and shift your attention to one of the others. The screaming in your ears, the screaming in your house, the screaming feeling of this book in your hand, the sight of the soft font of every single letter forming words. Slow everything down, block out the noise, breathe in deeply through your nose, count one… two… three… four… five… Now pause, then out slowly five… four… three… two… one… Now repeat. Feel the loving air being drawn up your nose, as your chest fills with hope… close your eyes and repeat. What you are feeling is like a powerful panic attack of hopelessness, but the fact of the matter is, you are very in control, my friend. You think, you believe, you know for sure… you're in a dark place. But you are the light in the dark; you are not anything anyone says, nor are you what you believe you are. You are truly a gift to this world, and if only you loved yourself, truly loved yourself, you'd see. You're more than enough, you have love to give, and you'll shine in this world.

There are so many lifelines you have, my friend. When thoughts feel relentless and you feel like you're backed into a corner, the art of distraction is a powerful tool.

Watch a show that makes you feel something. I could suggest watching a comedy, but if you're not in the right frame of mind, try this trick instead. Sit in front of the TV with your mind lost in thought, the sounds echo around the room as white noise, the screen blurs into faded shadows. Let that voice in your head watch it for the laughter, the jokes, the slapstick or the one-liners. Hone your attention on the setting, the costumes, the body language or ask yourself, how has the director filmed this? Are the actors doing a good job? Are there any mistakes that you can see? Life is a game; we have to deal with so many negative things, but distractions cause us to shift our attention and look at things differently. And when we do, we see things from a different perspective. It's like driving a car, focusing on the traffic, the road signs and listening to the navigator telling you which way to go. But then you get into a taxi and actually have the chance to see all the wonderful things along the road, which you never knew existed. "Oh… I've never seen that before!"

> *Life is the same; open your eyes*
> *and look beyond the darkness.*

Write your feelings down, even if it's just one sentence. Scribble. Cry. Scream into a pillow. Text a friend. Cuddle a pet. Walk outside. Eat something. Drink water. Just do something that shifts focus from one thing to another. These aren't solutions, but lifelines. They're ordinary actions that carry you from one moment to the next. And sometimes, getting through a moment is everything.

You don't need to have hope to stay alive, and you don't need to believe that things will get better, yet. You just need to give yourself the chance to find out. Another thing you need to know is that it's not about going forward, it's about... moving. A small side step, whether left or right, doesn't matter. It's a slow process, full of hard days, but also small and beautiful wins. And doing it by yourself can make it seem very hard, but there will be moments when you laugh again without faking it. When you feel the sun and realise you're glad you're still here. When someone says, "I'm so glad you stayed," and you know they mean it. These moments are waiting for you, so give yourself the chance to reach them.

You're not a burden.
You're not too much.
You're not beyond help.

You're a person in pain who's lost a little bit of love, compassion, and healing. You're someone whose story isn't over yet. Stay... take up space... be loud.

Please pick up your phone any time of day or night, and reach out to a stranger who is here, in the now, waiting to listen to your pain, without judgment, without blame, but with hope. They may not have a solution... just yet, but they will steer you in the right direction of a new tomorrow. They're trained to listen... and this is worth everything. Having a person to listen, sitting with you in the darkness, without needing you to be anything other than exactly who you are... YOURSELF.

Please don't let this be the end of your story. Please give the world more time to show you what else is possible. You're more than your darkest thoughts, and you're not alone... not now, not ever.

I'm glad you're still here, you keep me writing. If no one has told you today you matter more than you know, I'm telling you. The world is better with you in it, and I need you to keep going.

20. Parents

This section cuts deep, it's emotional, and I hear you!

The best place to start is by explaining what a parent is, and what they SHOULD do.

To begin, a mum or dad are the people who made you and brought you into this beautiful world. You are a gift and you have love in your heart.

A beautifully packaged individual!
I'm not wrong! You are! ♡

Please forgive me for using the term 'child.' I know you are reading this and you feel like you're a mature teenager, but in terms of safeguarding, you're still 'labelled' as a child. The global concept is that anyone under the age of 18 (or 19 in Korea) is considered a minor, which essentially means someone who has limited experience in the world and requires guidance in making decisions about laws, voting, and activities such as banking or driving. Depending on where you live, each country has specific laws that state when a child becomes an adult.

In simple terms: Parents are the people who SHOULD take care of you from the time you're a baby until you grow up, and even after that, too! They might be your biological mum and dad (the ones who gave birth to you), or they might be adoptive parents, stepparents, or even grandparents or other family members who take care of you like their own child. What makes someone a parent isn't just biology; it's how they love, care for, and raise you.

I will use the term 'parents' to cover all carers who look after you. Sometimes, children go to live with people who are not family; sometimes this is temporary, sometimes it is not. Regardless of the type of family you have, parents have a significant responsibility. They are the first teachers you ever had, and they help shape who you become as a person.

Parents Keeping You Safe

One of the biggest jobs your parents have to do is to keep you safe. When you were a baby, you couldn't do anything by yourself; you couldn't feed yourself, walk, or even talk! Your parents SHOULD make sure you have food, clothes, a warm place to sleep, and someone to hold you when you cry. Even now that you're growing up quickly, they SHOULD still make sure you're protected. That's why they SHOULD hold your hand when you cross the street, SHOULD make sure you wear your seatbelt in the car, or say no to things that could be dangerous. Sometimes it might seem like they're being too careful, but it's because they love you and SHOULD want to keep you out of harm's way.

Parents Tell You Right from Wrong

Parents SHOULD help you understand the difference between good and bad behaviour. When they tell you to be honest, to share your toys, or not to hit when you're angry, they are teaching you important lessons about being a kind and fair person when you become an adult. Sometimes you might make mistakes, and that's okay! That's part of learning. A good parent SHOULD help you learn from your mistakes instead of punishing you harshly. They SHOULD explain why something was wrong and SHOULD help you figure out how to do better next time.

Parents Help You Grow and Learn

Your parents SHOULD make sure you go to school, do your homework, and keep learning new things. They SHOULD help you read books, practise maths, or explore new hobbies like drawing, playing an instrument, or riding a bike. Even when they aren't teaching you directly, they SHOULD help your brain grow by talking to you, listening to your questions, and SHOULD encourage your curiosity. Parents SHOULD help you believe in yourself, so you can try hard things and not give up.

Parents Give You Love and Comfort

Everyone needs love, especially children! Parents SHOULD give love by hugging you, saying kind things, spending time with you, and being there when you're feeling sad or scared. If you've ever had a bad day at school and your parent hugged you or listened to you talk about it, that's them being a loving parent. Love isn't just about hugs, though. Love also means your parents SHOULD care deeply about you, even when you're having a tough time or acting out. They SHOULD love you no matter what; that's called unconditional love, and it means they SHOULD keep loving you always.

Parents set rules (even if you don't like them)

It's true, parents make rules, and sometimes those rules can be annoying. You may have a bedtime, curfew, screen time limits, or rules about finishing your dinner. You might wonder, "Why can't I do whatever I want?" Well, rules aren't there to make you miserable; they're there to help you grow up safe, healthy, and respectful. If your parents let you eat candy all day or stay up until midnight, you wouldn't feel very good after a while! Rules help guide your choices and teach you self-control. Good parents SHOULD explain the reasons behind the rules, so you can understand why they matter. And even though you might disagree with them all the time, rules are part of how your parents show you that they care.

Parents Support Your Dreams

Have you ever told your parent what you want to be when you grow up? Maybe a scientist, an artist, a football player, or a doctor. Parents SHOULD love hearing your dreams and want to help you reach them. That's why they SHOULD cheer you on at games, encourage you to try new things, or SHOULD help you practise the skills you need even when things become difficult. A parent SHOULD believe in you and SHOULD remind you not to give up. They're your biggest fans, and SHOULD always give you support to succeed.

Parents listen (even when you're upset)

Everyone feels angry, sad, or confused at times, even grown-ups. Good parents SHOULD listen when you're feeling those things. You can talk to them about your feelings, and they'll help you understand what's going on and how to deal with it. You don't have to be afraid of sharing your feelings with your parents. They are there to help you through it, not to make fun of you or tell you to "just get over it." Listening and understanding are also part of their job.

Parents Help You Become the Best

At the end of the day, your parents SHOULD want you to grow; this doesn't mean you have to be perfect. It means guiding you to be kind, brave, honest, curious, and strong. Parents SHOULD help shape your future by guiding your heart and mind. They do all this not because they have to, but because they want to. Raising a child is hard work, but it's also one of the most rewarding things anyone can do.

I hope you could tick most of the points above, and that you are happy and safe in the place you live. You have a right to all of the above, but I want you to understand some parents sometimes forget to see you.

It's Not Supposed to Be Like This!

Sometimes, people say, family is everything, but what if your family makes you feel small, scared, or like you're never good enough? What if the people who are supposed to love you… yell, hit, blame, or ignore you? This is a lot of negative stuff to take in.

Now let's go though some of the issues. You might wonder: 'Is this normal?' 'Am I just too sensitive?' 'What if this is what love looks like?' Let's be honest, it's <u>not</u> supposed to be like this. You shouldn't feel unsafe in your own home. No one should be hurt, humiliated, or left out on purpose. If it has been happening for a long time and no one sees it, or if no one believes you, it's not right. You have the power to recognise it. You might feel small, but you are big!

*Your voice is big, your actions are big,
and your heart is big.*

Surprisingly, many children are unaware that what they're experiencing is wrong. They don't speak out because they think everyone's like this. It's only when they get older and start interacting with other people that they begin to question what was happening. And even then, depending on several factors, which we will discuss later, they may still not say anything. I hope you understand that things may not always be as they should be. When you say to yourself, "This isn't right," you start to be in control!

But, at the moment, you might not feel safe enough telling anyone. It's okay. You have begun to make a change, and I'm proud of you!

Maybe your parent scares you. Perhaps you're worried no one will believe you. Maybe they said, "Don't talk about what happens in this house." That's okay… This chapter is for the quiet part of you, the part that's paying attention, even when your mouth stays shut.

*You are allowed to see what's happening.
You are allowed to protect your heart.
Even if you have to stay quiet for now.*

I don't know how many times I have said this: 'Stay under the radar!" But, how?

Here are a few quiet ways to protect yourself when you can't speak up, yet. I know it isn't easy. I know it might feel frightening. I also know that you may not have a safe place to store things or any privacy. But, there is always a way, and I know you have a big heart.

Keep a private truth list (for your eyes only). Write down what exactly happened, how it made you feel, and what you wish had been different. Hide it somewhere safe, or, if you feel your list might be found, you can recite it in your head. You could begin writing stories with code words, like yelling: "Storm voice." Lying about you: "Blame game." If you're being left out, "Invisible again." (We will talk about 'siblings' in another chapter). By writing hidden stories, you're observing what is happening. You're telling yourself you're not disappearing.

This helps your brain remember: You're not making it up. This is about you, and what a wonderful person you are. Even if you feel that you make mistakes sometimes, it is okay. These are your inner shields, as strong as steel. No one can break them down. Just thinking about them helps protect your heart.

You can tell yourself:

'This is not about me.'
'They're choosing to act this way.'
'I don't have to believe what they say.'

I know it's difficult to trust people, but I want you to be cautious with what I'm saying.

'Trust' is a huge word. It doesn't mean you can trust a person just because they have spoken to you or smiled at you. It's not someone on your bus. It is not just any adult, who you think, because they're older, they're going to listen. It's someone who cares, someone in your school, maybe a female teacher, dinner lady, librarian or neighbour. Those close to your parents might not be the best choice, but you are the best judge in these matters. But you don't have to say anything, yet. Remember, if you don't feel ready to talk, take your time.

Keep writing, keep remembering.
You're real! You're seen! You're important!

You shouldn't have to ask yourself:

"Maybe this is just how parents are."
"Maybe I deserve this."
"Maybe no one else talks about it because it's normal."

But here's what you need to know:

Just because something is common doesn't make it okay.
Just because it happens a lot doesn't mean it's right.
Just because grown-ups act like it's no big deal doesn't mean it's safe or fair.

These things are never okay, even if they happen in your home all the time:

X Being hit, slapped, pinched, or shoved. No one's allowed to hurt your body on purpose.

X Being called names like 'stupid', 'lazy', 'worthless', or 'cry-baby' Words can hurt just like hands. You don't deserve that.

X Being blamed for everything. You're not the cause of someone else's anger.

X Being ignored for hours or days. Love isn't supposed to feel like a punishment.

X Being compared to siblings in hurtful ways. You shouldn't have to fight for attention or love.

X Feeling afraid to speak, make a mistake, or just be yourself. You deserve to feel safe in your own home.

X Being told to keep scary or confusing secrets Anything that causes you harm should not be kept a secret.

Other people choose their actions. You are not responsible for their choices, and you didn't make them act this way. Having a home life isn't just about surviving; it's about being in a safe, friendly environment where you can grow, learn, and be loved, for all your good and all your flaws. You deserve to be loved.

Maybe you grew up with shouting, slamming, name-calling, or favouritism, which might feel confusing when someone tells you it's wrong. You might even feel bad for thinking it's wrong. Don't feel bad, you should be upset for having been lied to all of your life.

'Why am I treated like I am small, scared, or sick when I'm at home?'

'Why does my chest feel tight when I am at home, and can I breathe again when I go out?'

'Do I feel like nothing I do is ever enough?'

It makes me want to cry that you have to ask yourself so many questions, but these are clues. They matter and most importantly you do too.

What parents should do when you do something wrong is: they tell you off, take away your phone, make you apologise and then ground you for a bit. Next, is the awkward talk about what you learnt from the mistake, that you should not do it again, respect your parents, and the rules that they have set for you. There are several factors that may alter the order or severity of punishment, including culture, upbringing, or external influences.

Suppose you have to do chores to earn kindness, look after your sibling to earn playtime, or earn the right to have fun. I'm sorry to tell you, this isn't love.

This is building to the hardest question of all. "But, what can I do? I am just a kid?"

Your feelings are real. Your hurt is real.
Your story deserves to be better.

21. When love hurts!

The word 'love' is so beautiful, but trying to give it a real definition is confusing in itself. When a person says they love you but they also scare you, it raises many confusing questions: How can they tuck you into bed one night and yell at you the next? Well, you know the answer to that… it isn't love! Being in a family, sure, has its ups and downs, but when it's used like a weapon, in the form of pain, punishment, and fear, it gets twisted: It's not love.

If someone says "I love you" and then screams and pulls your hair, it's a strange way of showing they love you. You might still love them. Of course, you do; they're your parent. You can remember good times, such as hugs, bedtime stories, and the days when they smiled at you. All come at no cost to anyone. Okay, bedtime stories every night might be a difficult one to do every night, but the others?

That's what makes this so hard. It's the conflict of actions and words that make home life confusing.

Conflicting ideas that don't make sense:

'I love them.' vs *'They scare me.'*
'I miss them when they're kind.'

vs

'I feel small when they're mean.'

It feels like you want to scream - but if they love me, why do they treat me this way?

It is a complicated question; sometimes, they never learned how to love without hurting. Sometimes they don't even know they're being unkind. And sometimes... they do know, and choose it anyway.

The last one is the most hurtful. But none of these reasons make it your fault, and certainly none of them make it okay. Love that hurts, isn't safe love.

If we look at it from a different perspective:

Being a parent is difficult.
Being a parent is a job.
Being a parent is a struggle.
Being a parent is a 24 hour, 365 days a year hardship.

They all sound horrible, don't they?

Some parents view it this way. Instead, they should be looking at what brought you into the world.

Being a parent is not difficult.
Being a parent is an excellent job.
Being a parent is not a struggle.

* Being a parent is a 24 hour, 365 days a year gift. But, sadly, a lot of parents get wrapped up in their own struggles.

If this doesn't make sense to them, they don't deserve to have an amazing person like you in their lives.

Blaming difficult jobs, struggling to make ends meet, while working far too much, they don't stop to think what they're losing. They are losing you! I hope you... no, I hope *THEY* dare to read this chapter. I genuinely hope they realise what they are letting slip away. You'll soon be a beautiful young adult and move on to university. I know you are struggling at the moment, but patience is your friend; hold on. I know you have a strong heart, and you will get through all the hardships. However, the time will come, and hopefully your parents will realise it before it's too late. You will go soon enough and make a life for yourself. I know you may be in a tough environment, but please have patience, my friend.

You Don't Have to Choose Between Loving

Them and Protecting Yourself.

It's not disloyal to protect yourself. It's not wrong to feel sad, angry, or confused. You are not being unfair. You're being honest with yourself. You're allowed to say:

'I love you, but I don't like how you treat me.'

'I care about you, but I need space to feel safe.'

If someone says "I love you," but it doesn't come with:

Listening, Speaking, Caring, Apologising, Protecting, Noticing, Seeing, Watching, Observing.

It isn't love.

Love has no boundaries: No conditions, No limitations

Work is important, food is important, water is important… but to love your child is more important than any of these. Yes, a parent needs to provide, but if the sacrifice is you, then that isn't a sacrifice worth making.

You are growing up, and one day you'll get to choose how you treat others. You'll get to be the kind of person who never makes anyone feel small. You'll know what safe love looks like because you lived without it, and still grew kind. That's your power.

You don't have to become like them.
You get to become someone better.

In the next chapter, we'll talk about how to protect your heart when things at home feel too big, too loud, or too hurtful, and how to stay safe in small, quiet ways when you can't change the grown-ups around you.

22. Why Do They Blame Me?

If your mum or dad has said something is your fault, you might be feeling confused, scared, or even like you're a bad person. This is a hefty load to carry.

But still, you might wonder, "Why did they say that? Why would my parent blame me?" This is a really good question, and it deserves a gentle answer.

"But What If They Say It's My Fault?"

"You made me hit you."
"You talk too much, that's why I yell."
"If you were better, I wouldn't have to do this."

They may also use misdirection to confuse you even more: "You have anger issues, not us!" The whole thing is about questioning what you did (if anything). Never ask yourself, "What if?"

Now, I'm sorry for being so direct, but you deserve to know the truth. You can't turn back time… life moves forward. What is done is done!

Nothing can undo what has happened. It's about them, not you. Even though it's not fair, sometimes people choose to blame the person who's right in front of them. And when that person's you, hearing hurtful words doesn't make it true, even if it's coming from your mum or dad. They're supposed to protect you, not the opposite. But sometimes, when they're in a lot of pain themselves, they can make mistakes. Big ones. It might be because they're dealing with their own guilt, or because they don't know how to handle what happened. They might even feel angry at themselves deep down and not know what to do with that feeling, so they point it at someone else. This doesn't mean they don't love you. But it does mean they're not acting in a loving way.

In *Shadows Chant*, Aeona's mum refused to love Aeona. She rejects her. I truly hope with all my heart that your parents are not even close to the way Anwen treated her daughter. Hopefully, Anwen will see her outbursts for what they were, and have regret and remorse for what she did.

Love means keeping you safe. Love means telling the truth. Love means saying, "I'm hurting, but I still care about you." If your parent can't do that right now, again… that's about them, not you. Anwen should have been given special counselling for grief, to let go and forgive, but she just couldn't. It seems strange talking about forgiveness here, because there was no one to forgive.

A dictionary definition clearly says what it means - *Accident*: (noun) 1. an unfortunate incident that happens unexpectedly and unintentionally, typically resulting in damage or injury.

"She had an accident at school." *Similar: mishap, misfortune, misadventure, mischance, unfortunate incident.* 2. an event that happens by chance or that is without apparent or deliberate cause.

Did Aeona deliberately turn the gas on?
Did she intentionally make Nyxa disappear?
Did she purposely want to harm Fluff?
No… of course she didn't.

If someone is blaming you or making you feel unsafe with their words, you don't have to keep that secret. Talk to a teacher, counsellor, or trusted grown-up who can help you. Sometimes, a parent might… hopefully… eventually realise they were wrong to blame you. They might apologise… Sometimes, they never do. This brings us to 'forgiveness.'

Two things need to be considered here. First things first… Aeona needs to forgive herself, as discussed in the previous section. Still, we'll say here that it's a very difficult thing for a teenager to do. An accident was what it was… an accident. Sometimes our brain re-enacts what happened, and in doing so, our mind can add things that never really happened. Our brain can be silly like that, sometimes.

Our mind can also delete important information from our memories under the stress of the event. This is okay, as it's built like that to protect itself. Either way, accidents happen. Aeona didn't know she was going to step onto her cat's tail.

We need to talk about another difficult question… How can a person remove something hurtful that a parent has said?

I'm sorry, but when someone says hurtful words, it can take a very long time for them to go away, especially if it's from a parent. This is different from having to forgive yourself.

In the next chapter, we'll talk more about how to take care of your heart by learning to forgive yourself because even when other people say hurtful things, you can choose to be gentle with yourself. If you keep wondering: "Is it me?" You're starting off on the wrong foot. It's never about you. When home doesn't feel safe, your mind starts asking questions. Not once, but over and over again. If someone yells at you in a way that makes you shrink inside, makes you feel ashamed of who you are, or slaps, hits, or hurts your body in the name of "teaching you a lesson" … It hurts me to tell you, this isn't discipline, that's not love and that is certainly… never okay. Parents sometimes don't stop and think about what they're doing. Instead, they blame and start to become physical; this behaviour is unacceptable. You are valued, important and never small! If anyone begins with, "How long have you had anger issues?" They are certainly not looking after your best interests, and remember what I said earlier about whom to trust. These people aren't on your side! Find someone who will listen to you, because you're important and you need to be loved.

But here's the truth: every person is in charge of their own actions.

No matter what you said, no matter how messy your room is, no matter how angry they get. They choose to treat you like this. And that's about choice.

You didn't cause the storm,
you're just standing in the rain.

23. Gradual distancing

You want your space and privacy, where no one interferes with what you want to do, but no one seems to understand. It can be so infuriating! This time in your life marks the beginning of a transition towards independence and self-identity. It's normal for you to feel like this. You're on your way to becoming a responsible, self-sufficient young adult. You start to question your parents' ideas and reasoning behind what you see as silly rules. Their authority doesn't seem logical at times, as it starts to conflict with your own values and opinions.

Please don't feel that you're wrong for wanting to express your opinion, but remember, they are your parents. I know, a parent forcing their opinion on you can be annoying, especially in a world that doesn't make sense. This often prompts you to spend more time with people your own age, rather than with your family. Other people start to play a bigger role in your life, by giving you what appears to be a sense of belonging. It also helps you explore new aspects of your own personality.

Now comes the pinch. Firstly, be careful not to become attached to people older than you. It might seem rewarding, but they may entice you to do things that can spiral out of control and take you down a dark path. Just because you think they understand what you're feeling, doesn't mean they have your best interests in mind. Also, when parents notice that their once talkative child now shares less about their day or seems more interested in messaging friends than family dinners, they generally misinterpret this as a personal issue and will try to fix you. Not that you're broken, but some parents may think that you have a problem. It's good that they care and have taken the time to notice a change. Please try talking to them, without shouting or grumbling, and engage in a two-way discussion about what you're feeling. Simply put, being honest, as embarrassing as it may seem, puts your cards on the table. What many teenagers forget to see is that their parents were once teenagers, and may have done exactly what's troubling you.

Distancing doesn't mean cutting off or abandoning your family. It's about creating space to explore autonomy within your family. Things that may help involve setting boundaries, expressing opinions, and negotiating rules, often with some conflict along the way. These disagreements are part of the learning process for both you and your parents. They give you the chance to practise communication, assertiveness, and decision-making. For parents, it's a time to adapt, moving from a role of direct control to one of guidance and support. Well, this is what's supposed to happen.

Another big, big problem nowadays is technology. Although it allows you to connect with friends and discover interests independently while browsing the internet, it can hinder the connection you have with your parents. Some buy their child a phone, but others might say: "You're too young," or "Having a phone will distract you from studying!" or "The internet is full of bad stuff," and so on, and so on. Either way, it's not about you proving you're responsible to have one; it is more to do with trust they possibly lack in themselves. A significant amount of conflict between parents and children stems from this topic.

You may not have a phone, which is okay, because although you won't agree, phones and technology can widen the communication gap between you and your parents. If there isn't a balance with meaningful offline interaction, the atmosphere and silence in your home can be deafening. The occasional lonely laugh can be heard when someone scrolls onto something funny, but their laughter isn't shared, and they barely raise their head from the screen.

Please try to be kind to your parents. I know you feel pressured, punished or victimised, but they too can experience sadness or fear of you growing up. It may not feel like it, but before you open your mouth, and another shouting match begins, understand the emotions of those around you. It may help you navigate through the choppy water.

> *A shout, upon a shout,*
> *turns into background*
> *noise, with neither side*
> *listening to the storm.*

Another tricky thing to manage is when your parent begins to micro-manage everything you do. They control every decision, over-schedule activities, and constantly check in with your whereabouts. This obviously makes you feel like you are being suffocated. Am I wrong?

They don't understand that what they do is counterproduct-

ive. You will begin to push back at some point, either more aggressively or emotionally withdraw from them.

Parents who struggle to loosen control often do so out of love and concern for their child's well-being. But, they fear that without their 'control' you will make mistakes, fall in with the wrong crowd, or drift away completely, as discussed above. But what they don't understand is that their excessive control can backfire. It erodes trust, fuels secrecy, and makes you less likely to share your struggles. Instead of growing in confidence, you may become dependent, anxious, or rebellious. A healthy transition requires your parents to recognise that letting go doesn't mean you're abandoning them, but rather giving you the space allows you to grow, while they remain available to offer guidance and support.

Ultimately, gradual distancing isn't about growing apart but about growing differently. If you're allowed to take appropriate steps away from your parents, while still feeling loved and supported, you're more likely to develop a stronger sense of self. At this important stage in your life, you can build a better bond for the future. It feels like I am talking to the wrong person. If you ever get the chance, leave this book open on this section. Hopefully, they will pick it up and read some of these points. If your parents don't understand that it's better to calm the fire now, and have some solid ground to get over the rough patch with you, they may be faced with a 'burning bridge' in a broken relationship. There are times when you feel your life is like a wobbly bridge: uneven and shaking. Wouldn't it be wonderful if your parents held your hand, rather than sitting on different shores, looking at the burnt remnants of the relationship you both had?

24. Dealing with Sibling Favouritism

What do you do when it feels like your parent always chooses your sibling over you? They may smile more at your brother or sister, but frown whenever they look at you. They cheer loudly when your sister wins something, but barely even notice when you share something good.

"Why can't you be more like your brother?"
"Why aren't you like your sister?"
"Why are you always like this? Look at him."

Moments like these can sting so much. They can make you feel like you're invisible, or like no matter what you do, it's never enough. You might start to feel angry, confused, deeply hurt and wonder:

"What's wrong with me? Why can't they love me the same?"

Here's the most important thing you need to know: you're not the problem. You're not less lovable, too emotional, too quiet, or too loud. What you're experiencing is the pain of being compared unfairly by someone who is supposed to love you without conditions. This isn't your fault. It's them struggling to understand that you are different from your sibling, and that's okay!

You're going to be the best at anything you do and so much more! You're one of the most incredible things to ever come into this world. You've got a beautiful mind, and you're going to use it to create some wonderful things!

I believe this, and so should you.

Whether your parent stops believing in you or shows more love to your brother or sister, please stop listening to their negativity. What they say hurts, and I know it's hard, but it does not define who you are or what you are capable of. You're going to try to be better, but you aren't doing it to be seen, or noticed, or to show off. Think about it… what's the point? You'll only be raising their expectations until they set them so high, they'll be setting you up to fail, anyway.

You are going to do it for you! And you alone. It is not a competition. You're not hiding in your brother or sister's shadow; you are the bright light causing it. Lift your chin up, hold your head high and be proud of all of your accomplishments, however small.

Aeona went through the same as what you may be dealing with. Her mum favoured her twin brother, Christopher, which was more hurtful. However, her father saw them in the same light. Although he did treat her more gently than her brother, this is different from favouritism: she was his little princess. It's natural for fathers to treat girls a little softer, kinder, and daughters are usually closer to their father. But, it may depend on culture. (Read more in Between Two Worlds)

Favouritism can be blatant. One sibling is constantly receiving praise, hugs, help with homework, comfort, defended, and given the benefit of the doubt in conflicts. You, on the other hand, have to take up the slack. You're met with cold stares, criticism, endless chores, blamed for everything and told to toughen up if you let a tear slip out.

If this is happening in your home, you're not imagining it or being dramatic. It's not how families should work. It is unfair, and most importantly, your pain is real.

You might wonder why parents play favourites when they're supposed to love all their children equally. The truth is, favouritism usually has nothing to do with who the children are and everything to do with what's going on with the parent. It might feel like they relate more to one child than another, or it might be that you're a girl and he's a boy, or the other way around. Your parent might be uncomfortable with emotions they don't understand, so they pull away from the child who shows them. Sometimes, they punish a child who reminds them of someone from their past who caused them pain, a separation or divorce. This sometimes happens when families break up. I didn't say it was right. I said it can happen.

'You look like your dad.' or *'She looks like her mum.'*

Some parents try to put their children into roles. One child becomes the troublemaker or the difficult one. You are not a label. You are a complete and beautiful human being, with your own light, thoughts, emotions, and values. Sadly, your parents might not look beyond your complex exterior.

So, that brings us to the sibling. Are they to blame? It's a difficult question, only they can answer. Did they throw a spanner in the works or play one parent against you? It happens. They have the choice to accept the way the parents are treating you. Unless they're under four years old, they may be unaware of what's going on. However, if they pull tongues or give you that "I win" glance, now that's another hurtful thing you may have to deal with. On the other hand, if your sibling is aware, they can and should do the right thing and stand up for you.

Sibling rivalry

No rift should come between a brother or a sister.

Blood is truly thicker than water.

Don't let your parents force a wedge between you!

25. What If I'm Afraid to Tell?

When you're hurting at home, people will say, "Tell someone." But, it's not as easy as that, is it?

If you've thought about telling someone and then immediately stopped yourself, imagining all the ways it could go wrong or worse. "What'll happen if I speak up?" "What if it breaks my family apart?" I hear you, I'm very sorry you feel this way. Lying in bed at night and thinking, what if it's not even bad enough to ask for help? What if this is just what families are like? Lying in bed at night with questions keeping you awake isn't easy, either, but they are pretty standard. Your fears are real, and you're not alone in asking them. But here's something important: Even if you don't know where to start. You're allowed to speak up, even if your voice shakes.

Why Asking for Help Feels So Hard?

Sometimes, the person who hurts you is someone you love. This makes it really hard. However, being yelled at and hit, to the tune of, "This is for your own good," or "You made me do this," is not okay. Deep down, you know something isn't right. You need to understand, my friend, that asking for help isn't disloyal. It's not attention-seeking. It's brave. It's smart. It's how you need to protect yourself.

What makes a grown-up safe?

They should be someone who listens without interrupting. They believe and support you by helping you figure out what to do next. It could be a teacher, counsellor, librarian, coach, or youth worker. It might be a neighbour, your friend's parent, or an aunt who understands the family situation. How to start is a tough one, saying a little bit can open a big door.

You could start with something like:

'Something's happening at home, and I need advice.
'My parent is always angry.
'I think I'm being hurt at home, and don't know what to do.'

These opening questions are crucial for gaining an understanding of whether the person is the right one to talk to. However, "Can I tell you something, and will you keep it secret?" is different. By asking this question, you're putting the person into a very difficult corner. You must understand that the person you tell cannot promise to keep it a secret. If they feel that YOU are in danger of being physically harmed, they cannot keep it to themselves. Perhaps you require specialised assistance, or they lack the necessary knowledge or experience to help you in this type of emergency. However, please remember that you've taken a very brave step in speaking out.

If it feels too scary at the moment, there are other ways to ask for help. You can write a note or a message and pass it to a trusted person, or get a close friend to do it. You can draw how you feel. You can talk quietly or just whisper… "Can we talk?"

It's not a question of: What if they don't believe you? There's nothing wrong with speaking your truth. Do you think anyone's going to believe Aeona about her dragon? Think about it… Your truth is more believable than hers! Wait for *Shadows Chant II*, there are going to be a lot of surprised people.

If they say they don't believe you, it can feel like a punch in the stomach. You might think, "I knew I shouldn't have said anything." But that person's reaction doesn't make your truth any less real. It doesn't mean you were wrong to speak. It just means you talked to the wrong person. I can't say I'm sorry enough if this ever happens. But, please pluck up the courage to speak out again. Be proud of yourself, not ashamed. Never doubt, never question what the truth is. It may make you feel small and obviously hurt. Please gather your thoughts and regroup. While you wait to find another person, there are still things you can do to take care of yourself.

What happens after you tell?

Now, we will identify some things you may not like. I'm telling you as it is, which means you're going to have to make some difficult choices. It may also change your outlook on whom to talk to, but all of this is for your own good. It's tough, I'm not going to lie, it might be a lot to process. I know you held your breath when you read the above. It's okay to be nervous, but remember that your happiness is the most important thing here. You need to feel safe, be cared for in the right way, and be loved.

***

If a parent is hurting you, it can seem confusing and even scary to know that a counsellor might call the one who is doing it. You might wonder, "Aren't they supposed to protect me? Why would they tell the person who's hurting me?"

Here's what's going on behind the scenes, and as brutal as it sounds: you need to know what will happen.

It's a counsellor's duty to protect you by following specific rules. They're required by law to follow certain procedures, which are meant to keep children safe, but from your point of view, they're not what you'd expect. In some cases, these rules include contacting a parent or guardian, especially if:

You're under a certain age (often under 16 or 18).
You ask for help that requires action (like moving schools, missing class, or reporting abuse).
You disclose something that must legally be reported.

In serious situations, counsellors must report what you say, but not just to your parents, to several other people as well. If you tell a counsellor that your parent is hurting you physically or emotionally, they might be required to report it to Child Protection Services, a school safeguarding lead, a social worker, or a designated authority. Depending on where you live, the process may include informing your parent that something has been reported; however, that doesn't mean they will disclose everything you have reported to them. It is the authorities who decide how and when to inform the parent, especially if it's unsafe to do so immediately. This is supposed to protect you from further harm. Sometimes, the counsellor calls the parent because they don't realise how serious it is.

Remember, even if you have done something your parents didn't like. I can't say it plainer than this… there's a line that shouldn't be crossed. Unfortunately, not every adult understands the difference between strict parenting and abuse. What can make matters worse, is if a counsellor doesn't have all the details, or if they underestimate your pain, they might think, "I should let the parent know something's wrong," without realising it could make things worse.

This is why you <u>must</u>… (I know it may feel like you are betraying your parents) but… You <u>must</u> say exactly what's happening.

This is why it's really important, when you can, to report the incidents clearly. If you think by telling the trusted person, things will become more dangerous for you, be direct, saying:

'I'm scared to go home if they find out I've told you.'
'If you tell them, I'm afraid I'll get hit or worse.'
'Please don't call my parents. I don't feel safe.'

Even saying these things once can help a counsellor realise they need to be very careful. It is their job to keep you safe, not to protect the parents' feelings. You need to know that the counsellor's priority is always your safety. If you feel the counsellor didn't listen, or told your parent without protecting you, that's not your fault. You have the right to ask for another adult, a different counsellor, or someone who will hear you fully. I'm deeply sorry if this has happened to you. Please be strong, my friend.

You must ask:

'Can I understand what will happen before you tell anyone?'

'Can we talk about what's shared and what stays private?'

'Is there a way to get help without my parent knowing, yet?'

These questions aren't disrespectful; they're smart and brave. You deserve help without fear.

Every situation is different, but the trusted person should try to help. They may ask you to speak with someone who has experience dealing with similar issues. They might report what you've said to child protection services if you say that you're in danger.

They may even prevent you from going home if they think you are in real danger. The steps detailed above depend on your location, the severity of the situation, and the type of assistance available to you. This may sound a little too scary, but I know you're old enough to hear this. I'm telling you exactly how it is, you need to know your rights, but also the responsibilities of others who are trying to keep you safe, even if it feels like the complete opposite at times.

If I Tell a Teacher,
I'll Be Hurt More When I Get Home.

I am very sorry to tell you this, but… the truthful answer is: we don't know. Your fear is very real. And sadly, it's something many children go through on a daily basis. If you think that telling will lead to more pain, you have every right to protect yourself. Please check the back of this book for international Child Protection telephone numbers and websites. Protect yourself, my dear, use the internet responsibly when searching for services or helplines. If you're frightened at home, maybe leaving a search history of these may not be the brightest idea.

A word from Aeona

To my dear, beautiful friend,

I see you.

I see the way you've kept going, even when your heart is heavy. I see the way you've held your feelings inside, hoping someone will notice. I see how hard you try to be "enough" for someone who's supposed to love you just as you are. And I want you to know something, with all the love I have in me: it's never your fault.

You aren't too much. You aren't too hard to love. The way they treat you isn't a mirror of your worth. It reflects their own hurt, fear, or failure to love. But their blindness doesn't make you invisible. Their anger doesn't make you a bad person. Their silence doesn't mean you don't deserve to be heard. You are always enough, even when they can't see it.

You don't have to carry their blame anymore, and you don't have to earn their love. Your home should be filled with care, kindness, protection, and peace. You and I aren't perfect, because we shouldn't have to be.

I believe in you. I also believe in the bright future that's waiting for you, a place where you are seen, heard, and loved. Quietly, hand in hand, we're walking to tomorrow, even if you can't feel it yet.

Keep growing. Keep choosing kindness. Keep remembering who you are.

With love that will never disappear,

Aeona ♡

26. Divorce or Separation
Stuck in the Middle
Coping with Parents

When your parents decide to separate or divorce, it can feel like the ground beneath you is falling away. One day, everything seemed normal, and the next, your whole life changed. But I may be sugar-coating this a little. You're probably well aware of your mum and dad's relationship breakdown, so I'm not going to say it any other way than it is. You've felt the tension, the anger in the thick air, and possibly the general deterioration in communication. If it's already gone beyond making up and being a family, you must understand, before we talk about you being stuck in the middle, that it's not about you. Plain and simple, you are not the cause of the split.

Let's presume it's already happened. You might have to live in two homes, have split holidays, or see one parent less often. You feel caught between two people you love, unsure of where you belong. Being in the middle of your parents' conflict can be confusing, painful, and exhausting. Next, you probably already understand that from the day your parents went their separate ways, your life has changed, and there's probably nothing you can do about it either. You can try and try and try, but it's you who has to deal with the situation as best you can.

This guide isn't about telling you how to feel or pretending that everything's fine, because you are already reading this. It's about giving you space to understand what's happening, how to take care of yourself, and how to stay steady when everything around you feels unstable. Whether your parents' split is recent or happened a while ago, your feelings matter.

What is the difference between separation and divorce?

They are major life changes, and at their core, separation is usually the first step, after the continuous fights and arguments, where your parents can't seem to get along anymore. It's generally a long-term decision where your mum and dad live apart without ending a marriage, legally. Whilst 'divorce' means they've decided they can no longer stay or repair the damage in the relationship. In some places, marriage isn't seen as necessary, so two adults live together and raise a family without being married. Either way, whether married or not, the terms "separation" and "divorce" are often used interchangeably in these types of relationships.

This change will mean you have to cope with several changes, including moving to a new place, having two bedrooms, or adjusting to one parent no longer living at home. It might mean different schedules, new routines, or seeing one parent less often than you want to. It is a lot to take in all at once. Every family handles it differently. Some parents stay friends and work together. Others argue and struggle to communicate. Some parents keep you informed about what's going on. Others don't tell you much at all. The critical thing to understand is that even if your family is different now, it's still your family. The people who love you still love you. You didn't lose them just because their relationship with each other changed, although it may feel awkward at times. We can't talk about Aeona and her family here, but Anwen and Thomas loved the twins dearly; they still went through some rough patches of arguments and fights. Some parents go through these to show their children how much they love them. Depending on how old you are, sometimes your mum and dad make sure not to put their children in the middle. This is what parents should do, as the way your mum and dad love each other has nothing to do with the way they love you. Some children don't even know there is any trouble between their mum and dad, until the end.

Why do parents separate or divorce?

When your parents split, one of the hardest things can be not knowing or understanding the reason why. They may have kept their problems quiet as discussed above. Perhaps they fought in front of you all the time. Either way, you might be left with questions they can't or won't answer. Some teenagers start to wonder if they caused it.

Did I do something wrong?

Did they fight because of me?

The answer is always no.

Separation or divorce often occurs because of problems between the couple, not because of any issues you may have. Relationships are complicated, and sometimes people grow apart, argue too much, or can't agree on how to live together. Even if you were ever mentioned in an argument, you didn't cause the breakup. They are responsible for their choices, and their decision to separate is about them and not your actions.

In trying to protect you by hiding the truth or sugar-coating things, some parents don't understand how confusing or left out they can make you feel. Other times, they share too much, and you might feel like you're being dragged into scary drama. If either happens, it's okay to put a boundary between you and them. You can say you don't want to be involved in their arguments, and worst of all, being asked to choose sides. You'll probably never get any answers to why it happened, but one thing you can hold onto is this: you aren't the reason;

you didn't break their marriage. And I know you want to do all you can, but it's not your job to fix.

How It Affects You

Separation and divorce change how you feel, how you think, and sometimes how you act. You feel like you're on an emotional rollercoaster: one moment relieved that the fighting has stopped, and the next, you're missing the way things used to be. There's nothing wrong with having mixed emotions about it all. It is disturbing and can be quite terrifying for some of you, being in the middle of trench warfare with your hands over your ears, waiting for the white flag. You may also start noticing that things that didn't bother you before suddenly do: small things like comments from a friend or a change in routine can feel more intense than usual. That's because your brain and heart are adjusting to a major shift in direction. There's no timeframe for how long it is going to take to feel okay again, because remember, you lived in a home with both mum and dad, but once the home dynamics change, so do you.

School might also be affected; you can't focus, or your motivation has disappeared. You can't be bothered and continuously ask yourself, "What's the point?" Avoiding friends is another thing that you might see happening, not because you don't care, but because it feels easier than explaining what's going on at home. You're dealing with something really hard. If you do tell your friends, they should understand how tough it is. Some teens take on extra responsibilities, such as helping with younger siblings, cleaning, tidying, or doing the laundry, but burying yourself in chores or overexerting yourself may just be masking the hurt you feel.

Please remember, it's not your job to fix things or take care of everyone's emotions. You're a teenager, and you deserve to be supported through this, too. Some people may say, "comfort your mum," or "comfort your dad." Depending on the situation and whether you know the reasoning behind the breakdown, comforting mum, dad or both has to be handled very carefully. They both love you; this isn't the question, but if this becomes worse, it may be seen as choosing sides, even if you do feel closer to one parent over the other.

***

You're angry, upset or glad the fighting has ended. Finding ways to express what you're going through is tough. The same with everything, screaming, shouting because you're angry, and so you should be. Some people write letters they don't send, keep a private journal, or make a list of their emotions, but if you want to scream, you have every right to. Grab a pillow and go for it. If you have trouble sleeping, headaches, or want to be alone, you are reacting to the stress of the situation. It is tough, but try to treat yourself with kindness. Do things that will help you sleep, such as exercising. Please don't skip meals and make sure to drink enough. These small things can help you feel more in control when everything else feels upside down. With support and time, believe me, you'll find your balance again. What's happened or what is happening doesn't define who you are; it's something you're going through, and you have every right to deal with it at your own pace, in your own way.

I am sorry for everything you are going through, but once it has gone beyond the point of no return, you need to understand what the term 'custody' means. I'm being direct with you because you need to hear it. You are a young adult and understand what is happening. Living Arrangements may have to be handled with care. When parents separate, one of the most significant changes is figuring out where you'll live and how much time you'll spend with each parent. This is where custody comes in. There are different types of it, like… sometimes one parent has full custody and you live with them most, if not all of the time. At other times, custody is shared, and you alternate between both homes on a schedule. Some families switch every few days, while others alternate weeks. Some create plans based on school, work, or other responsibilities. This will likely make you angry, as the whole situation is confusing and emotionally charged. Some arrangements can be simple, with weekends with Dad and weekdays with Mum, but then if parents begin arguing about who has who on what day, it can be like trying to learn a new school timetable thrown into your already puzzling life.

You might not like the idea of leaving your room behind or adjusting to two routines. It may feel like you're constantly packing or as though you're living in two separate lives. You might feel closer to one parent but walk on eggshells with the other, trying not to hurt their feelings.

You have the right to discuss your custody situation. You're allowed to speak up. Depending on your age and local laws, your opinion might be considered when custody is decided. Even if your parents and the court ultimately make the decision, it's important to talk to someone about how you feel and what matters the most to you.

But what can I do?

Custody affects more than just where you sleep. It can influence your time with friends, your school routine, and your connection with extended family, such as grandparents, uncles, and aunts, as everyone has their opinion on what happened or who was to blame. While you may not be able to control every detail, you can still create consistency by establishing your own habits and routines that follow you. A special journal, playlist, or weekly video call with a friend can help you stay grounded.

The most important thing to know is that custody doesn't change who you are. You are not defined by where you stay or how often you see each parent. You're still loved, valued, and worthy of stability, even when things feel uncertain; your voice matters, and your well-being should be part of every decision made about your life. You don't have to pick sides because you're allowed to love both of your parents. What happens between them doesn't change the fact that they're both part of your life, and that both of them can care about you in their own ways. Love isn't a competition. It's not something you should ever have to ration or defend. Some teenagers worry they'll lose connection with one parent or feel like they're being pulled apart emotionally.

It's also common to feel invisible, as if your needs and voice are being overlooked in their decisions. The situation may not be something you asked for, but your response to it matters. Your feelings are valid and deserve to be heard. Please don't be hard on yourself, you didn't ask for any of this.

You begin to see relationships in a different light. This is a very important issue that we need to address. When your parents break up, it's between two people who have either lost love for one another or something has happened between them, not you. This isn't the norm; it's okay that it happened, and you didn't play a part in it, my friend. This doesn't mean that any relationship will break down. Your outlook on two people together is one of love and trust. A lot of teenagers fall into this trap and say, "I'm never trusting anyone," or "I'm never getting married." Life doesn't work like this. You need to understand that some people stay together, while others don't. There are many reasons for people to stay together, but there are also many reasons why relationships fade. So, seeing your parents separate can make it harder to trust that love lasts or that families stay together.

You may feel uncertain about what to expect from others or worry that relationships always end in pain. These feelings are real and deserve attention, but they don't have to define your future. With time and support, you can create your own understanding of what healthy, respectful love looks like.

Being affected doesn't make you weak. It makes you human. You don't have to handle all these emotions on your own. Talking, writing, creating, or simply being around people who care about you can be part of your healing process. What you feel matters, and you deserve the space to feel it without judgment.

27. Between Two Worlds
When culture hurts.

Suppose you come from a family with a strong cultural background, whether your parents were born in another country or you're part of a tight-knit ethnic or religious community. In that case, you've probably noticed that things at home might be different from how some of your friends live. This can be a wonderful thing: be proud of who you are, and never let anyone say otherwise.

To the colour of your skin, hair, eyes, every minute detail, not forgetting your beautiful heart and even the way you think.

Inside and out, you are unique.

Where you're from and your culture bring beautiful things to the world: language, food, faith, traditions, and a deep sense of belonging. You have so much to share and offer. Talking with your friends and discovering different things is so rewarding, but sometimes it throws up surprises that you're unaware of.

What appears to be normal to you, might be alarming to others.

They may have different ideas about discipline, control, and other experiences of parenting that can sound and feel confusing, especially when you're growing up in a world where people are talking more openly about wellbeing, children's rights, along with mental and emotional health.

You might wonder:

Is what I'm going through normal?

Why does my home feel different from others?

Let's explore these questions without judgment and without putting yourself at risk.

Culture Shapes How Parents Raise Their Children

In many families, parenting is deeply connected to culture. In some communities, strict discipline is viewed as necessary to raise respectful and responsible children. Parents might say, "This is how we do things in our family," or "This is how I was raised."

In other places, there may be a greater emphasis on explaining rules, avoiding punishment, and discussing issues openly. Both approaches stem from places of love, but they can feel very different to grow up in, especially when interacting with your friends. You will find some differences that don't make sense. But, as we've already identified, there are many cultural variations in how to bring up a child, whether for the good or bad.

For example, in some homes, being yelled at is a common and often considered everyday occurrence. In others, raising your voice is deemed inappropriate. In one family, being hit with a shoe or belt might be regarded as part of discipline, while in another, even a light slap would be called abuse. These differences can make you question your own surroundings. If everyone around you seems okay with it or even says it's part of your culture, you might feel confused about whether your pain is real.

Culture doesn't cancel out emotion.
We all feel. Your feelings matter,
even if others don't understand them.

If you're growing up with parents from one culture while living in a country with different values, you might feel stuck between two sets of expectations, which can be really hard. Outside of your home, you may see your classmates talking openly about their parents, setting boundaries, or being allowed to make mistakes without being punished harshly. Meanwhile, at home, you might be expected to obey without question and never show weakness. This creates something called cultural dissonance, when the beliefs you're raised with don't fully match the world you're living in. And when it comes to discipline, this dissonance can be especially painful.

You might feel invisible, ashamed, or like you're betraying your family just for thinking differently.

You're not betraying anyone. You're just trying to make sense of a complicated situation, and that takes courage. You may ask yourself, "But I feel like I'm torn between two worlds." Many teenagers in this situation start to doubt themselves or feel like they're being too sensitive for feeling hurt. You might even feel guilty for wishing things were different at home. Perhaps you've been told that you're acting like an outsider and being disrespectful simply because you disagree with specific house rules.

'You should be grateful.'
'You don't know what real hardship is.'
'Other kids would be thankful to have a roof over their head.'

This can leave you feeling ashamed for even questioning your experience. But here's the thing: It's okay to feel hurt. It's okay to feel confused. And it's okay to wish things were better, even if your parents are doing what they believe is right. When you're constantly trying to balance loyalty to your family with your own emotional survival, you end up carrying a weight no teenager should have to carry alone. Then everything builds up, and you start to feel the pressure of staying silent.

Another thing is that in many cultures, family comes first above everything else. You may have been raised to believe that what happens at home stays private and that loyalty means never discussing family problems with others. This can make it extremely difficult to express your feelings. Even if something hurts, you might keep it inside because you don't want to bring shame to your family, or they don't want you to 'make a scene.' Speaking out means you are choosing sides: between your culture and your wellbeing. This is an impossible choice for you, but many teenagers face this dilemma every day. You aren't the only one going through this. Many teens from immigrant families or culturally strict homes feel the same way: trapped between love and fear, respect and silence, tradition and the need to grow. Sometimes, speaking with someone from a similar background or country can be helpful. Just asking, "Do your parents ever go too far when they're mad?" or "Do you ever feel like no one would understand what it's like at home?" can open a conversation that makes you feel less alone. They may be in the same year at school, or in the year above you. It is better if they are a little older than you. But, be mindful of the questions you ask!

Instead of asking them directly, you can pose a general question in a safe group setting, for example, "In some families, parents discipline their children by taking away privileges, others shout or even get physical. What kinds of discipline are common in your country?" Avoid direct personal questions like: "Do your parents hit you?" as it may feel confrontational, invasive and may trigger distress.

Remember, this isn't about pointing fingers. You are reaching out for understanding or emotional support. You're beginning to gather information to help you understand that love shouldn't come at the price of your emotional safety. You can honour your parents' intentions while still being honest about how their actions affect you. It doesn't have to be either/or. Growth can live in the in-between. This invites cultural reflection, not personal exposure.

To get a better understanding, you could speak to a grandmother or grandfather about how you feel. However, if you're not ready or unable to speak up, that's okay. You can still take care of yourself in quiet, meaningful ways. If it's safe to do so, write down your thoughts and feelings. Even just writing, "Today was hard," can help your heart release the stress you're carrying. Find trusted spaces, such as a school, a club, a community centre, or a quiet spot outdoors, where you feel grounded and more like yourself. Set tiny mental boundaries, even if you can't say it. Thinking "This isn't okay, and it isn't my fault" is a powerful way to care for your inner self. If you ever do decide to reach out for help, you won't be starting from zero; you'll have already begun the most crucial part: understanding what's happening and believing in yourself.

When things are extremely tough and another day begins just like it'll end... in tears. You have to protect your beautiful heart because, at the moment, it feels like you're stuck in a vicious circle of cultural pressure. You go to school with a heavy heart, already not in the mood for studying or seeing your friends... what's the point? The clock ticks through the day, but your head is still spinning from the screaming turmoil of your morning routine. A drone of noise buzzing in your ears and teachers pointing at the board. As the last lesson edges towards certainty, your chest begins to tighten, your breathing becomes laboured... it's home time. For others, smiles, cheers, hugs and handshakes, but you glance left and right, wishing you could feel the same. Your friends go quiet because they understand, but all they can do is gently give you a pat on the shoulder, in solemn support. "There's nothing I can do?"

It's not the best option, nor is it a solution to what you're going through, but it can build a wall of mental and emotional protection around you. Practice having two heads. One for home and one for the moment you step out the door.

Let's look at your day again.

Every day, you go to school with a heavy heart, already worn out and not in the mood for studying or seeing your friends… STOP! From now on, it's going to be different.

You wake up to the screaming and rapid fire like you're the reason their sleep has been disturbed, or your brother hasn't put his shoes on, the laundry is still in the washing machine, and you haven't done the urgent chores that will, for some reason, determine their life. You're crying because you want to go to school or bury your head under the pillow, hoping for it all to go away. Fat chance of that happening. I am very sorry your 'home' feels like a continuous war zone of friendly fire, and your young life is the collateral damage. You can't stop it as much as you try, but you can thicken your skin, turn off or zone out.

Time for school. You finally push yourself out of the door, already tired from the onslaught. The door, a solid barrier behind you… If only there were silence outside, but your heart is pounding in your chest in fury. At this point, try to close your eyes, breathe deeply through your nose and out of your mouth, counting down… five… four… three… two… one. Now you are going to remove your 'HOME-HEAD' and replace it with your 'YOU-HEAD'

Now, when you leave the house, tell… no force yourself to say, "Here I am me! I'm leaving my troubles here." Your friends miss you. You miss yourself. Affirmations like this can help you deal with the mornings. "I'm going to have a peaceful day." And "I'm going to smile, a real beautiful smile to light the day." Your friends still know what happens at home, but by doing this, you aren't carrying the hurt of home throughout the day. You need to give your heart and mind a rest.

It may take some time to understand the importance of this, but please, my dear friend, stick with it; you owe it to yourself.

When the clock ticks through the day, your head will slowly stop spinning, and the drone of white noise will settle. As the last lesson edges towards certainty, keep the smile on your face, you know your 'HOME-HEAD' is waiting for you on the doorstep.

Be strong, even on the dark days,
you're tougher than you think.

28. Impermanence
The World Keeps Turning

Aeona was eight years old when her world came crashing down. Her home. Her parents. Her brother. Once wrapped in warm hugs every day, and then everything, in the flick of a switch. All she knew - gone in an instant. Imagine the heartache, the pain... the unbearable finality of it all.

Not because she wanted it to go away, but because her life altered into a piercing blue light. Waking up in a hospital room, staring at a white ceiling, unaware of where she was, listening to the distant drone of doctors and nurses faded into confusion. No one would explain what happened in a way that made sense. Well... not until she remembered the explosion. Luckily, she had no memory after that.

Faced with the painful realisation that nothing could bring her father, brother and her mother's love back, she was rejected and blamed. Yet even after the worst things she could imagine, the days just kept coming and coming. For Aeona, the sun still rose. The world didn't stop. One day blurred into the next, memory after memory, guilt after guilt and regret after regret.

I truly hope you never have to experience anything that shakes your world to the very core.

Impermanence is a painful truth.

Nothing stays the same forever, not in the bad nor the good. People leave. Homes change hands. Friends drift apart. Moments slip away like sand between your fingers. Sometimes, these changes come wrapped in confusion and pain that we saw coming. This is why understanding impermanence can be perceived as cruel. It makes us question, 'Why can't the things we love last forever?'

You probably felt the same way when you transitioned from primary to secondary school. Perhaps you kept some of your school friends to soften the blow; you may have changed schools altogether. It was a significant change in your life. It might have taken you a few weeks to settle into the routine of moving classes for different subjects. But, think about it, it didn't take you long before you stopped getting lost, learning to ask where a class was, or to become familiar with where you needed to be, at a particular time.

When life is good, impermanence is the farthest thing from our minds. When we're laughing, we don't think, "This won't last." You're in that moment, living it. Enjoy the great times, grab hold of them with two hands and wrap your arms around the happiness you have. Love what you have, let the memories burn into your heart. You deserve every second, because you are a beautiful person with joy in your heart. This is what helps soften the hard times. This is how change works: the happy times should be at the forefront of your mind, even when the problems seem too much. But the hurt can sneak in quietly, and before you know it, it overshadows the happiness, as if it never happened.

No matter how heavy today feels, tomorrow is still coming, whether we're ready for it or not. I could tell you that tomorrow will be a better day. You need to believe it will. The rollercoaster will hurtle downwards, but will come back up.

Some days acceptance comes easily, other days, not so much. There's hope, even if your heart feels like it's shattered into a thousand pieces. This is the start of a learning journey, not to 'get over' your losses, but to carry them differently. You still have happiness in your heart, but it just beats with a different sound, a different path to an improved you.

Giving yourself time to identify what's changed, even if you don't fully understand it yet, is a decisive first step. Say it out loud, or write it down, instead of pretending everything is the same. By doing so, you're admitting: 'Something is different, and I notice it.' This honesty takes courage. Once you acknowledge the change, permit yourself to feel everything. There is no "right" way to react. Some people cry for days; some go quiet and keep to themselves. Some become angry at the unfairness of it all; others feel numb, as if their emotions are frozen. It's okay to feel like this. Your feelings are not a problem; they're part of your process. It's okay to wish you could rewind, but wishing doesn't make you weak.

Carrying What You Can't Keep

This is one of the things about impermanence: just because something doesn't last doesn't mean it didn't matter. Sometimes, we think "moving on" means forgetting completely. We worry that if we talk about someone too much, or if we let ourselves remember them, we'll never heal. However, thinking about the past and building a future can occur simultaneously. You don't have to erase what hurt you to survive; you just have to carry it differently, just like we discussed in grief and guilt. The memories are what drive us to improve, and thinking about them can sometimes be seen as a positive thing, not a negative one. Healing doesn't follow a schedule. Some people around you will expect you to "be over it" in a short time, not because they want you to be better, but to stop them from feeling awkward around your sadness. It's true that nothing lasts forever, so this means the hardest days don't last forever, either.

You must try to reflect on what is happening. Look at yourself and ask, 'What is one thing that has changed in my life recently? Please take a moment to consider this. Has it affected you emotionally or mentally? Write down the specific feelings like: anger, sadness, relief, and confusion.

Is there something or someone you miss, but are too afraid to admit it? A friendship that ended badly, or a family member who moved away. Maybe it's a past version of yourself.

Next, write - why you miss them or it, and while you're at it, add what you're afraid will happen if you admit it out loud. Let your words be truthful and messy. Here is another question to consider: Picture yourself a few months or years ago, right before everything shifted - what would you say? Would any of your advice have lessened the impact of today? By listening to yourself answering these questions, you will begin to process what has happened and how it has affected you, emotionally and mentally. Ask yourself, what are three things in your life are good, right now, no matter how small they feel? Then, write a note to your future self. It could be something you are going through now, a lesson you are learning or a feeling you are holding on to. Use it as a promise to yourself: 'No matter what happens next, I won't forget…'

Suppose Aeona was walking beside you. What advice would you give her? As she is moving forward in her own story, you are writing your own. Life changes, sometimes for the better, sometimes for the worse. You change, adapt and learn. The joy, the tears and the heartache make you who you are. You may not be perfect, but you are perfection in the making.

29. Compassion and Self-Forgiveness

I call it a journey… others will call it a guide. I suppose it is, but I think it's more about opening your eyes and having a good look at yourself. Then, ask yourself one little question, 'Do I deserve all the pain I give myself?' Because, if you step back, I think you know the answer to that. It's when you take everything down to the bare bones that you see we all might be beating ourselves up with a stick, when we should be reflecting on its justification. It might not seem like it at times, but slowly… and step by step… You can move towards being content. Let's not jump to happiness, just yet. Maybe you can aim for, being able to sleep at night with peace in your heart. You might be reading this and think these things don't happen in my world. If this is the case, I want you to hold your hand on your broken heart, and make a promise to yourself. Aeona is going to try, and you are going to try to make things better. You might not know it yet, but there is so much you can both do. You deserve to be happy. Aeona deserves to be happy. And together, we ARE going to work it out.

You have come so far in reading this book and learning about some of the ways you have a voice. You will be heard, whether you whisper it, scream it out loud, or say it quietly in your heart. Whether you've faced hurtful words, rejection, loneliness, been shouted at, hit, punched, or been mistreated. Remember, you have a beautiful heart, and no one can touch that! Suppose you are reading this to offer support to your friends or even those around you, whom you have observed, while you are waiting patiently for them to pluck up the courage to reach out. May this guide bring you mercy, compassion, and self-forgiveness, even in the darkest of nights. Sometimes, words blend together without any defining border, and in the end, we think they are all the same. I want to discuss two key concepts: Compassion and Self-Forgiveness. They mean all the same, don't they? It appears that they have some significant differences.

All of them begin with you.

Compassion is about empathy, which is when a person has felt the same as you at some point in their life. It's about making a person feel better, listened to, and cared for. For example, if someone has lost a loved one, simply sitting with them can offer emotional support and strengthen their relationships.

Self-forgiveness is about your heart, releasing guilt, pain, or inner turmoil. For example, if you hurt someone and said 'sorry', this is very good. But saying it isn't the same as feeling sorry. For a person to be genuinely sorry, they must work through the guilt to find peace within themselves.

Compassion begins with lowering your phone to the world around you. The moment your attention shifts from the bright screen of your own worries to the quiet landscape of someone else's pain, everything changes.

Picture sitting in class just before lunch, half-listening to the teacher while also checking the clock. Out of the corner of your eye, you catch a classmate staring at their desk, shoulders hunched. Nothing dramatic. No tears. Just a stillness that feels heavier than the room. Most days, you might gloss over the details, but today something tugs at you. You lean a fraction closer, not enough for anyone to notice, but enough for your inner lens to sharpen. Noticing is compassion's first breath. This is what you look like some days. Lost in your own thoughts. Do you think no one notices? You will be surprised to know… They do. They may not even sit at the same table. They might not know how to approach you. At times, they may even be crying out for someone to notice them. But, generally, we're all lost in our own hardships, unable to see others.

For teenagers, life is often so loud, sport practice, exams, friendships flickering like neon lights, family voices overlapping, and this silence can feel like you're invisible. Yet silence often hides the backstory. The friend who suddenly ghosts the group chat, the sibling who answers in one-word grunts, the kid on the bus stop who always sits to one side. When you train your heart to notice, you begin to read these muted signals. Compassion doesn't just happen; it comes from seeing.

If you only see the frowns and the smiles, you are not looking hard enough. Beyond the outward appearance are the subtle changes in mood, body language or even posture. Having the simple thought: Something might be happening here.

Noticing… can be hurtful to your own heart.

You might feel awkward or afraid that the person might react aggressively or pull away. This is normal, but compassion doesn't demand perfect words; it asks for your presence. Sometimes, a soft "Hey, you good?" between classes. Sometimes it's just choosing a seat beside the quiet person at lunch. It might be sharing your charger without making a fuss. Tiny gestures form a secret code.

Over time, these codes will weave into safety nets… for you both, strong enough to catch a falling soul. Reading this extract from Chapter Five of *Shadows Chant* shows how a little compassion can build mountains of hope. Here, Nyxa notices Aeona's nervousness, pain and loneliness.

"Aeona went to the living room, still dressed in her pyjamas. At first, she didn't notice the girl sitting silently in an armchair in the corner, curtains drawn to block out the daylight. Distorted rays managed to break in from the uneven folds of fabric, concertinaed like a Spanish dress near the ceiling.

Aeona sat on the opposite side of the room until she saw the strange girl, then she frowned silently, trying to figure her out. Nyxa sensed her and subtly glanced up from her book, then lowered her eyes again.

"I like you," she whispered, without looking.

Aeona eased her frown. Nyxa glanced again to see if the young girl was still glaring at her.

The truth was that Aeona had never seen a girl like her before. Her deep, matte black lips parted, and the words drifted in a ghost-like breath. "You read," snaked their way across the room to Aeona. Thick liner framed her foreboding eyes, scanning rapidly left and right across the pages. And every so often, her hands wrapped around the book, a spider-like nail, long and sharp, painted in the same jet-black shade as her lips, would slowly turn the page.

Aeona pursed her lips, looking at the darkness as she mouthed the words. She liked them and imagined whether she would look as intimidating. She plucked up the courage, trying to imitate the girl's mysterious tone. "I can read..." she growled, shyly adding, "a little." It was clear that they were both testing each other, wanting to trust but neither wanting to let down their guard.

"You like playing with fire, too?" Nyxa tested.

Anger started to swell in the young girl. "Don't," she spat. Nyxa wanted to see how far she could go. "Don't what?" she asked, not raising her eyes from her book.

"Just don't!" This time, Aeona forced the words through piercing eyes.

The older girl continued reading through her book, showing no interest in the scorn thrown at her from across the room. Then she said something that threw Aeona off guard.

"It looks good on you."

Aeona couldn't think of anything to say, unsure of how to respond to the comment.

Beyond these initial moments, noticing becomes a skill you sharpen like a pencil. Imagine waiting in line for the cafeteria, head down, stomach growling, when a student at the front glances back, lips pressed in a tight line. The bell still minutes away, you have a split second to decide: do you keep your focus on the tray in front of you, or do you quietly ask, "You okay?" This small interruption can change their day, allowing them to breathe rather than brace for the next challenge.

Learning to notice also means noticing the unnoticeable: yourself. Sounds odd, doesn't it? But think about it for a second. You might be the one who feels invisible at times, lost in the crowd or awkward in conversation. Paying attention to your own inner self helps you detect similar cues in others. When you feel that hollow twist in your chest, you develop sensitivity toward someone else's same pang. Your own experience of isolation can extend your own kindness.

Once you start, you'll find you won't be able to stop analysing the dynamics of those around you: a friend who always speaks up in debates, the one who never gets a chance to voice an opinion, the two who whisper secrets behind closed notebooks. Watch how voices rise or drop. Listen for sighs, cleared throats, shifting postures. These subtleties are often conveyed through a person's body language. When you train yourself to read them, you step into a deeper dimension of care.

You may have just asked yourself, how does this help me?

Well, before you go to school or work, pause for a minute. Close your eyes and picture the people you are going to encounter: classmates, teachers, and the cleaners.

Send each of them a wish:

> *May you be seen.*
> *May you be safe.*

Then open your eyes and start your day. By doing this, it readies your heart to focus on the unnoticed.

Noticing the subtle shifts is an art. By paying attention to those around you, you can see what is really happening. Not only will you notice the hidden problems, silent suffering and hurt, but also the positive emotions. You deepen your empathy and you realise that everyone deserves compassion. Not all the time, but the more you observe, the more you will be able to notice the changes in people.

I understand that you might ask, "But what happens when you begin to notice too much and feel overwhelmed by what you see?" Compassion fatigue can soon follow. You have to remind yourself that noticing doesn't require you to solve every problem. You can't. It simply means acknowledging. If you encounter someone drowning in grief, you don't have to rescue them from every wave of sadness. Sometimes, just holding out your hand to keep them above water is enough. A small thing to say, "I see you," is all they need.

Another thing you may notice is a slight lapse in conversation.

Gaps between words carry meaning. If you sense someone is searching for the right moment to speak, ask to invite them in: "I am here. I am listening." You can also pay close attention to the tone of someone's voice, the crack of certainty, the tremor in excitement, the pause that holds unspoken fears. "Sorry for noticing" isn't an apology; it is a sign of deep listening. "But you sound frustrated," signals you hear them and are reaching out. This echoes in a cave of loneliness when a person feels lost.

Showing that your attention holds space for them tells them you have a beautiful heart. When Nyxa first saw Aeona, she quietly commented on her scars and in doing so, she opened the door for her. She said, "It looks good on you." But, really, what she was saying was, "I'm listening."

You'll also see little changes in your own heart. Pay attention to when you feel discomfort: if you feel resistance to helping a particular person, ask yourself, Why? Could it be fear of rejection, envy or past hurt? Noticing such barriers allows you to break them down. Compassion begins with awareness of those around you, but it flourishes when you start to look at your own heart.

If you feel up to it, why not start making notes? Each evening, you could write down incidents where you observed someone's unspoken emotions: a friend's drooping shoulders, a classmate's uneasy laughter. Adults around you also have their ups and downs. What about a teacher's tired sigh? Reflect on how you responded or might respond tomorrow. Maybe you noticed a person with sick days piling up. You could send them a message or email. If you aren't friends with the person, say to the person who usually sits next to them. "I see Sara isn't in again. I hope she is alright." Believe me, it will get back to them, because compassion is for all, not just your friends.

Please remember, this goes both ways. It's for kindness, your own beautiful heart and your own wellbeing. You might not think anyone notices you, but you'll be surprised who does. Finally, noticing is an act of courage. It makes you vulnerable to the pain you're witnessing.

When you first start to notice that someone is hurting, it's a little like spotting a shy kitten under a chair. You see that it has a problem. It is these little things that you have to look out for. Maybe your classmate keeps their head down all day. Maybe your younger brother slams his bedroom door as soon as he gets home. You feel a tug inside, the same way you might feel a tug on a string when a fish bites. That tug is the signal that compassion has woken up. But noticing by itself is only half of it. Now, to help, you need to bridge the gap between what you see and what you do. This space is the gap, and bridging it takes courage, patience, and a willingness to try even if you might mess up a little. In *Shadows Chant*, Nyxa had seen several children come and go from the home with Mary, but it wasn't until Aeona arrived that she saw that she was different. Compassion for the girl ate at Nyxa's heart. Please remember, compassion is distinct from pity. It is clear that Aeona had facial scars from the fire, but it was the sadness in her eyes that caught Nyxa's attention.

Many teenagers, younger children, and, honestly, adults, fall into the Fix-It Trap. It doesn't take long for both of you to fall. What you need to do is offer steady companionship by sitting with them. What you are saying is, "I'm here." You can share a memory, bring over snacks, or play a silly mobile game side by side for a while. These things aren't going to 'fix' what they are going through, but they may help them feel less alone.

30. Self Forgiveness
The Art of Starting Again.

An ordinary night can turn, the moment a memory arises like a blinding light in the dark. One second, you are scrolling through your social media, half-laughing, half-yawning; the next, your stomach drops as an image burns back to life: of the classmate you poked fun at, the photo you should never have posted, the desperate lie you told when the truth felt too risky or something worse. It can feel as if you are reliving the whole scene.

The first instinct is to swipe up, turn up the volume, and sink into the distraction of the following clip. Yet no matter how hard you try, running away traps you in a loop of what you have said or done. But, we can't generally say, "It is only a memory, it cannot hurt me now."

Our brain can sometimes do hurtful things by replaying hurtful things we have said or think we have said or done. Reviewing the event requires honesty, and with it comes the sting. But you're not the only one who thinks that admitting fault means you hate yourself, and denial is what actually fuels self-hatred. Fairness does not mean scolding yourself; it means creating a balance. This isn't excuse-making; it's thinking about the context behind what you said. Adding context helps reveal the moment when a different decision could have been made.

With Aeona, her world fell apart with a glass of water, but this doesn't mean she should punish herself for that simple act. Think about when you did something. You made a choice, whatever it was, it was a direction you chose to go. You cannot change what you did, you can't bring back what was lost. But you have hurt yourself enough. Time to let it go. Every minute detail, every sound, movement and word. You don't deserve this self-hatred. You don't deserve it at all.

Whatever you have done can't be undone. However, even now as you're reading this, courage is building within you, and you're ready to face the unsettling memory without buckling. By confronting a rough episode does not diminish your worth. You're a beautiful person who will continue to grow, because you deserve it.

Once you face a mistake, the question becomes:

What now?

The answer is not like a script we can learn. We usually say, "Sorry" quickly and hope it blows over. It usually does, but depending on what we do, the person may accept our apology… but it is not as simple as that, you see. We never learn to say "sorry" to ourselves, do we?

Standing in front of the mirror, gripping the sink until the pain from your fingertips feels like blood is going to come from your nails. You want to scream, but you are not alone. Your mum or dad will come banging… and to make matters worse, there are all the questions and a never-ending list of things from A to Z, on how to fix you… I think you can do without, "Now, you have to apologise."

Whether you are lying with the pillow over your head, sitting on the toilet with your phone in your hand, thinking of what to write, or standing in the bathroom with your thoughts, can feel raw. No one said it was going to be easy, apologising to yourself.

Mean what you say to yourself, "I didn't mean to hurt you." While it may be true or not, the only person judging you is you.

An apology has four main parts.

1. Apologising
2. Correction (if possible)
3. Apologising to yourself
4. 4. Self-Forgiveness

You say, "Sorry." They'll either accept it or they won't, but that's okay. You're holding your hand up, admitting that you were in the wrong. This is a brave act in itself… so well done if you have ever done this. It takes a lot of courage to take responsibility for our actions. Sometimes it turns into a screaming match or becomes physical. We sometimes act strangely; we would rather fight than accept ownership for our mistakes. I am not talking about accidents. This is a different type of apology. "I'm so sorry, I will be more careful next time."

It can be brutal when the other person doesn't accept your sincerity and remorse. The time frame of receiving the rejection is sometimes more painful than the event itself. This can be difficult to move from, but if it happens, you have to. The whole point of this is for you to accept you did what you could to make amends, and if you did this from the bottom of your heart.

You cannot deny yourself that. You cannot hate them for it, either. Of course, you may ask yourself, "Why?" But you already know the answer to that. I'm sorry, but you hurt them. And now you want to hurt yourself. "How?" you ask. By not being kind to yourself. Believe me, we blindly hold on to so much until it begins to cloud our hearts, and everything turns numb.

Becoming Your Own Ally.

Even after your honesty and attempt to repair the damage, echoes linger.

You could be laughing at break when, out of nowhere, a flash of memory strikes: the disappointed look or trembling voice of a friend burns back into your mind, as if replaying the scene. I'm sorry, but it happens. There's no delete button, no erase... just covered over by more memories, and hopefully, you can bring some closure to some of the bad ones. Try to soften the sharp gasp with a slow breath in through your nose. Think about how you'd calm someone down who's angry, distressed or having a panic attack. That voice in your head is always there to put you down, so try to push it aside. Many of you unknowingly let yourself be controlled by it. The voice in your head: snapping, being sarcastic, or being impatient, telling you to hurry up.

As you would change your ringtone or choose a different voice on one of your phone apps. Swap the critic for a mentor. Instead of it putting you down... Tell it, "I don't want to listen to you anymore!"

Sounds silly, but it isn't going to listen to you anyway. Now, here's the 'but': you try to make it give you pointers on what to do next time, instead of all the negative things it throws at you. A mentor voice will notice you made a mistake, but will change the way it addresses the issue: "Yes, that was dumb. Here is what we learnt from it." We all make little comments: we shouldn't, do little things and fall over once in a while. Please get up, that voice in your head is going to scold you anyway, but now it's going to give you pointers for next time.

We all hate it when people tell us, 'Calm down, breathe…' Relax, because that is all they have to offer. They don't hear the voice in your head or see it from your valid perspective. They talk and talk and talk, when sometimes you just want them to shut up. You have an internal battle going on, with that replay and voice in your head giving you a running commentary, and sometimes, you can hear yourself screaming in the background.

There are a couple of other things you can try. One reliable method to quiet that inner voice is the 5-4-3-2-1 scan: note five things you can see, four things you can touch, three things you can hear, two things you can smell, and one thing you can taste. This checklist pulls attention away from the echo, to the present. Another thing you could try is tapping with your right hand and then with your left, like a rhythm back and forth. By doing this, it focuses your brain on the now, rather than the past.

You're saying to yourself: I'm here. I'm learning. I'm moving forward. This helps to reassure ourselves with a physical calm.

As already covered in the other sections, writing about your regret, guilt, hardship and how you overcome them or thoughts that reduced the hurt. These are your small victories. When you begin to feel emotional about the past, read through a couple of your entries. Reading the concrete evidence of you forgiving yourself, or facing your difficulties like a champ, alters the dark voice's tendency to generalise your error.

You are no failure.
You are developing and becoming stronger as you
grow, you who can and will forgive.

Self-alliance involves managing your triggers. It's all about how a memory is connected to your emotions. But, you can replay the memory and take a different fork in the road. You can technically over-write it. Suppose a particular place reminds you of an argument, walk there first thing in the morning with a friend, chatting about something enjoyable, and making new memories in that space. If a song prompts regrets, pair it with a positive task. By changing and redesigning your triggers, you shift from being a hostage to hurtful memories. We learn from our mistakes; it is part of growing up. I know this sounds like a little cliché, but knowing you can handle the fallout makes us stronger. Fear loses its hold on you, because the worst-case scenario... messing up, no longer throws you into a black hole of remorse, regret and thinking you're a failure.

Reflect, Repair, Realign.

Setbacks will still sting. Handling it with a clear mind means you can have some predictable recovery. When a new mistake occurs, the steps remain: acknowledge it quickly, outline the repair, tap right and left for control, ask for help (when needed), and write it down. The faster you do these steps, the shorter the regret, guilt and remorse.

Letter from Aeona

Hi there,

I want to let you know I'm here. I see your gentle, brave soul reading this right now.

I know your pain, so I know there are moments when your heart feels heavy, when a memory stings, when you wish you could press rewind. I wish we could, but if only we can grow. I want to wrap you in kindness and remind you of two truths: you are deeply loved, and you can always begin again. When you catch that quiet voice inside you whispering, "You messed up," reach out to yourself like you would to a friend. Place your hand over your heart and say:

I'm sorry you feel pain. You deserve compassion and love.

Today is new. When regret tugs at you, breathe in deeply. I want you to forgive yourself. We cannot undo. But we can welcome what we create. You are precious, worthy of your own compassion. Whenever you feel lost, remember I'm here, proud of you for every step you take toward healing and hope.

With all my love,

Aeona ♡

31. Introduction to Happiness

I want to thank you from the bottom of my heart for getting this far. I know you and Aeona have cried along the way. Some hard and sometimes brutal truths have been discussed. However, with practice, you will be able to overcome the pain, and this will ultimately lead you to the goal of happiness.

It may seem a distant dream, just out of reach or at the very tips of your fingers, at times.

It is your right to have happiness, joy, peace, and to grow with love. Whether you have faced more pain, confusion, or hurt than you deserved. We are going to learn how to recognise and create it for yourself, lean on the people who care, face the fear that holds you back, and imagine a future where you are both the dreamer and the protector of your own heart.

A Happy Mindset ♡

First, we need to define: what it is and what it means to be happy. Once we know what it is, we can decide if we have it or not. Happiness is supposed to be a warm, bubbly feeling we get when things are going well, like when we're playing our favour- rite game, laughing with friends, or snuggling up to a pet. It's these moments when we feel joy, excitement, or content, and everything seems just right.

> *The feeling that you are a part of everything: home,*
> *friends, life, decisions, warmth, care and safety.*

We have covered some challenging topics in reading this guide. We have read about how Aeona has faced: grief, loneliness, guilt, and parents. So, happiness, warmth, bubbly, laughing, and snuggling may… have very little meaning to us, possibly in our present state. But happiness isn't only about fun times. It also comes from doing things that matter to you, like learning a new skill, helping someone else, or working on a project that makes you feel proud. When you see yourself getting better at something, whether it's drawing, riding a bike, or reading a book, you experience a deeper feeling that sticks with you.

If we are seeking happiness, we may need to look within ourselves, rather than relying on those who are supposed to give us love, care, and support. The people around us may think that they aren't giving us what they perceive as 'love, care and support', but for us, the bottom line is that we need to stop looking to other people to make us happy. Happiness comes from within and can be of our own making or from those around us.

Friends and family should also play a significant role in our happiness. Spending time with people who care about you, playing games, discussing your day, or simply sharing a joke, helps you feel loved and understood. Great, when they have your back, give you praise and are a shoulder to lean on. These connections give us support when we're feeling down and add to the fun when things are going… right.

Where to start? That's a good question.

Happiness often starts in our head. The way we talk to ourselves and look at challenges can either make our days brighter or weigh us down. As a teenager, you're juggling schoolwork, friendships, hobbies, and a whole lot of changes. Leaning your thoughts toward the positive can make us more confident, less stressed, and, ultimately, content, happy, or even happier overall.

The stupid voice in your head needs to be shaken off: "You're no good at this" when you face a difficult math problem, or "Nobody sees you" at break. These "automatic thoughts" are like dark shadows: you don't see them, but they sit… waiting to make your whole day feel gloomy. To catch them out, try this simple trick. In the evening, before bed, take five minutes to write down any negative thoughts you remember having in the day. Maybe you thought, "I'm terrible at spelling", or "Why did the teacher pick me out?" Writing these down helps push the voice to one side, and by getting it out of its hiding place, the negative thoughts are on the page.

It can put you down, it can poke fun at you.
But in truth, it is powerless.

We have already mentioned being less harsh on yourself in the section: Compassion, which is a good place to start. Being kind to yourself is just as important as talking positively. We're often nicer to our friends when they make mistakes than we are to ourselves.

Suppose a friend makes a mistake. You probably say, "It's okay, keep trying!" But when you do, you might scold yourself, "I'm an idiot." Try treating yourself like a friend, instead of your own enemy. Whenever you feel upset by making a mistake, place your hand on your chest and say quietly or in your head, "It's okay, everyone messes up sometimes." Remind yourself that making mistakes is a natural part of the learning process. If you want to go further, write a message to yourself, describing what went wrong, how you feel, and then end with a kind message: "It's okay, I learnt from it." Always a self-check… smile before a frown.

You may have also heard of something called Affirmations. These are short, positive things to say to yourself, which can give your brain a boost every morning. They aren't magic, they don't work immediately, but they're like little positive seeds you plant every morning.

Make them real and achievable. Instead of "I'm good at everything." Try, "I am going to have a good day," or "I am going to be more confident today." Stand in front of your mirror, look yourself straight in the eyes, and say it out loud. It might feel silly at first, but over time, your mind will start to hear your positive self, rather than the negative voice in your head. You don't even need to remember them; write them on a sticky note and stick it on your mirror, notebook, or the back of your bedroom door. We are slowly understanding what happiness is, and we are getting an idea of a few things that'll help change the way we feel about ourselves, which is a great start.

There is another concept called a 'Happy Mindset', which involves believing that we can grow and improve. If we think we're "bad" at something from the start, we shouldn't try new activities because we're scared of failing. However, if we believe that practice and hard work will help us improve, challenges will become exciting puzzles instead of intimidating obstacles. Let's think about this: when you are facing a difficult task, say to yourself, "I can't do this… yet," instead of "I can't do this." This little word, "yet", reminds you that with time and effort, you will get to grips with it.

Doing and trying is better than not celebrating at all. Each step you take, even if you fall, is proof you're learning, improving and growing. Try ending your day with a catch-up on affirmations. Look back at the notes on your mirror. You may feel a bit silly at first saying these things to yourself, and that's okay. This is about you and no one else.

'I am going to have a good day!'
'I am going to be more confident today!'

You looked yourself in the eye and make sure to use two important words: 'good' and 'confident.' If you do, you're already on the way to feeling better… keep at it. As the days and weeks pass, take note of how you're doing by keeping a simple "Better-day journal." At the end of each week, write one or two sentences about moments when you pushed away the negative voice in your head, battled with it and won.

You win some, you lose some.

Also note times you tried hard at something new and what you learnt, even if it didn't work out the first time, the second or the third. I am very proud of you for keeping at it. Over the month, you'll have a log of your small victories and hurdles you've overcome. Reading through your progress will show you how much you've grown and make you feel proud of your efforts. Remember… this is for you, your triumphs, your falls, and your loving heart. Growing a mindset doesn't mean you'll feel good every minute of every day. Bad moods, tough challenges, and mistakes will still happen, and that's okay. You can scream into a pillow and be angry sometimes. What changes is how you handle it. Please remember, you are the master of that voice in your head… never let it win. You have the controls, you want to be happy… and it doesn't like it. By noticing these unhelpful thoughts, being firm on your positive affirmations, treating yourself with kindness, and believing in your ability to grow, you're training your mind to overcome the negative and find hope and happiness more easily.

Building Strong Relationships

Now, this topic differs from the other sections: Sibling Rivalry, Parents, and When Culture Hurts. Connections improve for those of you who have to deal with issues in those areas. They say blood is thicker than water… I don't know how much truth there is in it either, nor who 'they' are, but we can hope it has some solid ground. Friendships and family connections are like the roots of a tree: the deeper and healthier they grow, the stronger you feel when a storm hits. As a teenager, you're learning who you are and how you fit into the world. Building relationships that feel safe from harm, fun without judgment, and respect for who you are, along with feeling supported.

*Knowing you have people in your corner
makes even tough days a little brighter.*

First, it's helpful to remember that having a few close friends is more important than knowing a large number of people. They are not real friends. People on social media aren't your friends. I'm not saying it's easy, but I know you might be afraid of letting people know about your fears, or some of the things you've been through, or what you're going through. It's not always easy to trust people, but please try to do so.

Aeona didn't have her brother to confide in, but maybe you do or a sister. Perhaps you are closer to one of your siblings or cousins than to the others, or maybe a distant relative, such as an aunt. Whoever it is… test the water, you might be surprised. When Aeona's brother left, Nyxa came into her life, and then she finally had someone to call a friend. Instead, look for the listeners when you talk, those who laugh at the same jokes, and stick up for you when things get hard. These are the people who cheer your successes and comfort you when you're down. If you don't have any friends, it's okay, but being down, if you have no one to lift you up, is a lonely road, and that voice in your head isn't going to pick you up. Please try. You might find them in your class, on your sports team, or in an after-school club. If you're not sure, quietly watch those around you, (Write the affirmation on your sticky-note, "I am going to be brave today.") By inviting someone who seems alone to work on a project or play a game, sometimes being the one to show kindness, can help you discover a special connection you didn't know was there.

Remember, forming a close friendship takes time, but once you've found someone who feels trustworthy, make a point to really listen when they talk. Active listening means giving your full attention, maintaining eye contact, nodding, and asking questions such as "How did that make you feel?" or "What happened next?" It's easy to think about what you want to say next, but when you slow down and focus on exactly what your friend is sharing, they know you care. When your turn to speak comes, you'll feel more connected because you've both had a chance to be heard.

Happiness is contagious. You and your new friend might talk about hardships, but through supporting each other brings connections which will lead to a better you. And this is a step towards happiness. Empathy goes hand in hand with listening. Expressing appreciation is another powerful way to strengthen bonds. Sometimes, we forget to say 'thank you' for the little things. Even Aeona sometimes forgot, we do when something unexpected happens or the gratitude is suddenly thrust upon us. In the story, Aeona was in the village, and an old lady gave her some money to get something from the shop, because she pretended that she didn't have any.

"No, sorry, but I seem to have forgotten my money." Aeona searched for a believable excuse, "I'd better go home and put that coat on as you suggest." She stuttered, looking at where to run. "No need, my love. Here, take this," the old woman reached into her purse, produced a pound coin, and swiftly pushed it into Aeona's hand. "Nip into the shop and get what you want quickly; run home, my love," she winked, waving bye with her walking stick, and off she walked.

When someone does something kind, like this, or invites you to sit with them at lunch, lends you a pencil, or says, "thank you", they make you feel appreciated.

You could even write a short note or send them a message: "Thanks for helping me today. You made it so much better!" Small gestures of appreciation remind people that you notice and value what they do, and they often encourage more kindness in return. In today's digital world, relationships can also grow online. But please be careful. Although it can bring happiness, it is short-lived, instant and may not last very long. Chatting in a group text or sharing a funny TikTok can be a fun way to stay connected after school. However, it's also important to maintain healthy online friendships. Make sure you only share information and photos you're comfortable with, and never feel pressured to reply immediately if you need a break. If you see a friend posting something that worries you, like mean comments or sad messages, reach out privately: "I saw what you wrote. Are you okay?" Offering a listening ear online can be just as meaningful as in person.

Taking Care of Your Body

Your body and mind work together like teammates in a bond of happiness. When you move, eat, and rest well, your brain gets the fuel and energy it needs to help you concentrate. Growing fast is what teenagers do: your bones, muscles, and brain are all in a phase of big changes. Please don't feel uncomfortable reading this. It's true, but we don't discuss it with anyone, so that's why it feels cringeworthy. Paying attention to how you treat your body now sets you up not only for feeling happier today, but also for staying healthy and strong as you grow and develop.

Of course, you're not going to agree with this, but the voice in your head and your phone are your enemies. We're all generally addicted to our phones, teens and adults alike. However, physical activity isn't just about participating in sports or going to the gym. It can be as simple as... dancing in your room, riding your bike, or helping in the garden. When you move your body, it releases chemicals called endorphins that lift your mood and give you a sense of calm. So, what I'm trying to say is: by doing literally anything that stretches your body and brings on a sweat, you can make yourself happy.

Sounds odd, but it is what the science says to support it. There are three chemicals which help us feel better: endorphins, dopamine and oxytocin. Usually, our brain releases them in a kind of sequence. When you first start moving or laughing, endorphins kick in to help ease discomfort and can help release some of that stress. Then, dopamine is released when you reach a goal or complete something, giving you a happy "I did it!" feeling. Finally, oxytocin shows up when you share that moment with friends or family, helping you feel close and connected. It's the endorphins which keep you on a high after break, if you're running around or playing with the other students. Please give it a try and experiment with different kinds of things, such as team sports and solo activities like skateboarding. Set your own pace; activities like dance, martial arts, or even hula hooping can help you connect with your body in new ways. Thirty minutes is the goal, but if you break it up into two 15-minute bursts, that's perfectly fine too.

I know that sometimes you don't feel like eating or overeat, but try to eat a variety of healthy foods. It provides your body with all the right ingredients to grow strong and think clearly. See, your body and your mind work together. Instead of thinking of "good" and "bad" food, try thinking about what's in it.

Vitamins and minerals that support everything from healthy skin to sharp memory.

Protein, found in nuts, beans, eggs, and lean meats helps build strong muscles and repair tiny "tears" in muscle fibres after a workout.

Whole grains, such as brown rice, oatmeal, and whole-wheat bread, provide a steady source of energy.

Fruits and vegetables.

Don't worry about being perfect, even if it's just a small swap. Apple slices instead of chips. All of this sounds terrible to me, but at the moment, if you are feeling down. Please give it a try. Food changes the way you think, the way your body works and the way you feel about yourself, inside and out. Remember, don't let that voice in your head put you down. All it takes is a fight back or going back to your affirmations. Why not make a new one? It may sound horrible at first, but start small and see how it goes. Another important thing is water. Your body is composed mainly of water, and every cell requires water to function correctly. When you're thirsty, it's a sign you're already a bit dehydrated, which can make you feel tired, drained or down. If plain water is boring, add something not too sweet, such as a slice of lemon or a few berries, to give it flavour. Try to limit fizzy drinks, as they give us a sugar rush. At times, we can have it, but with the highs come the lows. After the initial rush has passed, it can leave us feeling worse.

The next thing we're going to look at is a very tough topic to discuss with many of you.

Sleep

Mobile phones, social media, television, and endless shows. Are we all just scared of missing something? Not really. Many of us, including adults, struggle to make a conscious decision and put it down at the end of the day. It is addictive, whether you agree or not, that's fine, but one thing we all agree on is sleep. We can't deny that we need it to function.

Science indicates that different age groups require a specific number of hours of sleep. I won't include the numbers here, but they seem like an impossible task, especially given the way we live nowadays. The fact is that growing bodies need plenty of sleep to recharge. Like charging your phone, without enough power, you can't run at any capacity, let alone 'full'. Whatever the figures, establishing a routine can help your brain wind down. Try turning off screens (phones, tablets, TVs) at least an hour before bed. Read a chapter of a book or listen to music (not any music, but something to slow your thoughts down for the night). Also, having a dark room helps with settling in for the night. If you need a night light, choose one with a soft, warm glow that won't keep you awake. It is 'blue light' that affects our sleep because we're exposed to the first morning light, so our brain is confused about waking up, rather than the other way around.

We are still focusing on happiness. Now, you see everything we do is linked to our wellbeing. You are beginning to comfort, like, and eventually love yourself for everything beautiful you are. Looking at little things, one step at a time, you are moulding your heart into a better perception of what love is, rather than waiting for it to come to you.

Finding out what stresses you out is a key to being happy. Stress can hit you at any time; school, friends, or family issues can pile on, but being aware of triggers can lessen the damage and fallout.

Remember, everybody is unique. You might grow taller faster than another student, your stamina might be less, you might suck at math or science, but be good at English or the other way around. It's okay, please stop comparing yourself to people around you. You will get there in the end… and so

what, if you don't! Be happy with even the smallest wins...
That is real progress and happiness

32. Discovering Your Purpose
Setting Goals

Finding something that matters is essential. It might be tough at first to find something that makes you wake up with excitement, like a spring you jump out of bed. Think of purpose like a goal; it might be about art, learning about animals, or mastering a sport. When you find something that feels important, you can set goals that carry you forward, one step at a time.

Purpose often grows from noticing what you enjoy and what makes you feel proud. Start by remembering moments when you felt happy or energised. It could be the time you learnt how to ride a bike, or when you spent hours building something without getting bored. Think deeply; there may be a few, or if you feel that happy memories are a little difficult to find, consider setting some things you would like to do. It doesn't matter how impossible they seem, yet. Jot them down on sticky notes. Then, look at it. Do they have anything in common? Do you have anything creative or helping someone? Figuring out how things work? These shared themes point toward what you value, the things you care about most.

Once you've identified what matters to you, imagine where you'd like to be in a few weeks, months, or even years, as some of your goals might take longer to achieve. If you write down a long-term plan, take pride in yourself. You're setting something extraordinary, and as time passes, you can adjust the steps to achieving it.

No ifs or buts… go get it! The only thing stopping it is you. Things may seem impossible. Tell yourself:

No, doesn't mean, No!
It means, Game On!

Visualise yourself doing it and put the list somewhere you'll see it every morning, on your bedroom wall or next to your mirror. Seeing your dreams in front of you makes them feel real and reminds you why you're setting your sights on them. However, we know that big dreams can feel overwhelming, so breaking them down into small, manageable pieces is the key to steady progress. Instead of staring at a blank page, write one word in the middle. It might take you a few more days to write another word next to it, but you have to start somewhere, and if it's with one word… so be it… Excellent new ventures begin with one letter until they become a word. After a week or so, you might have ten words and begin to map the way forward.

That feeling of "I made this happen" is one of the greatest motivators. Aeona started with the letters the dragon saw… they made up a word… She began writing her own story with that single word – LAMBTON. And just like her, you will start to write yours.

Go Get Your Dreams! You have everything you need… in a single word. Think of it like a tiny seed in the palm of your hand. It doesn't look like much, does it? By giving your goals some structure, they become even more powerful.

Be: S-M-A-R-T

(Specific, Measurable, Achievable, Relevant, and Time-Limited)

If you like, you can simplify the words, but not the idea. You just need to ask the right questions.

Is this achievable?
How will I know if I am ready?
Can I really do this?
How will I ever have enough resources?
Why is it worth the effort?
When will I finish the first step?

They don't sound right, do they?

They certainly don't, because you are already setting yourself up for failure.

Try rewording them.

What is the best time frame to achieve this? (Depends on the goal.)

How do I measure my progress?

(One step at a time.)

What am I going to achieve at each step of the way?

(Each little goal has its reward.)

What are my key objectives at each step, to move on to the next? (Tick them off, review, regroup.)

How to raise the money and resources?

(A few small jobs, fundraisers, ecommerce, sponsored walk, etc.)

Also, if your questions need tweaking, alter them as you go along. They're not set in stone. If something steps in your way, rewrite the question. Have you ever thought it might be "the when" rather than "the what" that's stopping you from feeling happy? Happiness is finding the time to be happy.

Reflect on when you have felt happier doing something, and when you have been doing the same thing, but thought that you were forcing yourself to do it. This is what I mean by time. You may be a morning or evening person. You may be extra tired on a Friday after school, and then be excited that it's the weekend, but something feels off, and you're not in the mood. Keep a log of when you are happy doing a task and when you feel a little bored, tired or unhappy.

Be a detective in the little differences in your ups and downs. "What made me feel proud this week?" If, for example, you drew a picture, but it felt rushed because you had too much homework, you might decide next week to switch your sketch time to Saturday morning instead. By adjusting as you go, you keep your goals aligned with your real life, so they stay enjoyable instead of feeling like chores. If you can find someone who shares your passion, tell them about your weekly plan. Ask them to check in with you now and then, and compare the drawing. Knowing someone else shares your dreams adds a special boost. Sometimes goals outgrow their original plan. Maybe after drawing animals, you discover you love illustrating fantasy creatures even more than real animals. A wonderful accident, you never knew you had in you. It's good to update your vision to happiness. Remember, every little change is a development, and as you change, you are learning more about yourself.

A Final Letter from Aeona

My dearest one,

Do you know how proud I am of you?

You walk through sadness instead of running from it. You sit with loneliness under its cold umbrella. When no one's listening to your pain, you let your heart speak with love. That is what true courage looks like.

I know you don't deserve the blame that's being thrown at you. And I know how heavy it all must feel. But I have seen your light through every chapter. You may not feel like a hero, but I do, because a real hero isn't someone who never falls down. A hero is someone who gets back up with gentleness in their hands. I know you didn't ask for any of this.

I want you to remember: You're not broken. You're not too much. And no matter what happens next, you will rise above all the hurt. I will be right here, in the pages with a warmth that whispers: You matter. You've always mattered. Keep dreaming. Keep becoming.

Be gentle with yourself.

love

Aeona ♡

A Final Letter from the author

Dear reader,

You've walked through so much.

You've read about grief and mourning, about heartbreak and pain. You've looked closely at loneliness and felt the ache of being left behind. You've explored forgiveness, even when it felt impossible. You've touched mercy and compassion, and maybe started to offer some of it to yourself. You've dared to look at your parents and wonder why they couldn't always love you the way you needed.

And in the end... you're on the way to being happy. Not loud, perfect happiness, but the kind that grows slowly and softly inside you. Remember, this is no small thing. It's something very, very brave, it can also be something very, very scary. But, be proud of every little step you take. I truly hope you will find your place in the world. Smile because you want to, not because you have to, but in doing so... it is contagious.

Love who you are and smile with that in your heart.

You take care of yourself my dear one.

Paul Outram

TELEPHONE HELPLINES

Knowing where to turn for support can make all the difference. The resources below are here to help you, no matter what's on your mind. You're never totally alone.

The telephone lines are not exhaustive. Please reach out and find someone to listen. Remember, this is about finding someone to listen and give you some quiet advice. You can listen to what they're saying; there is no harm in this. Ultimately, you decide to learn, understand, or most of all, protect yourself and look after your heart.

You can stay anonymous, use a fake name or if you're in real need and would like them to take a more active role. Please be brave, strong, and take care of your own heart and wellbeing. And when you feel brave, please give them your name.

https://www.therapyroute.com/article/helplines-suicide-hotlines-and-crisis-lines-from-around-the-world

No matter where you are.

No matter what your pain.

Please reach out and speak to someone.

EUROPE

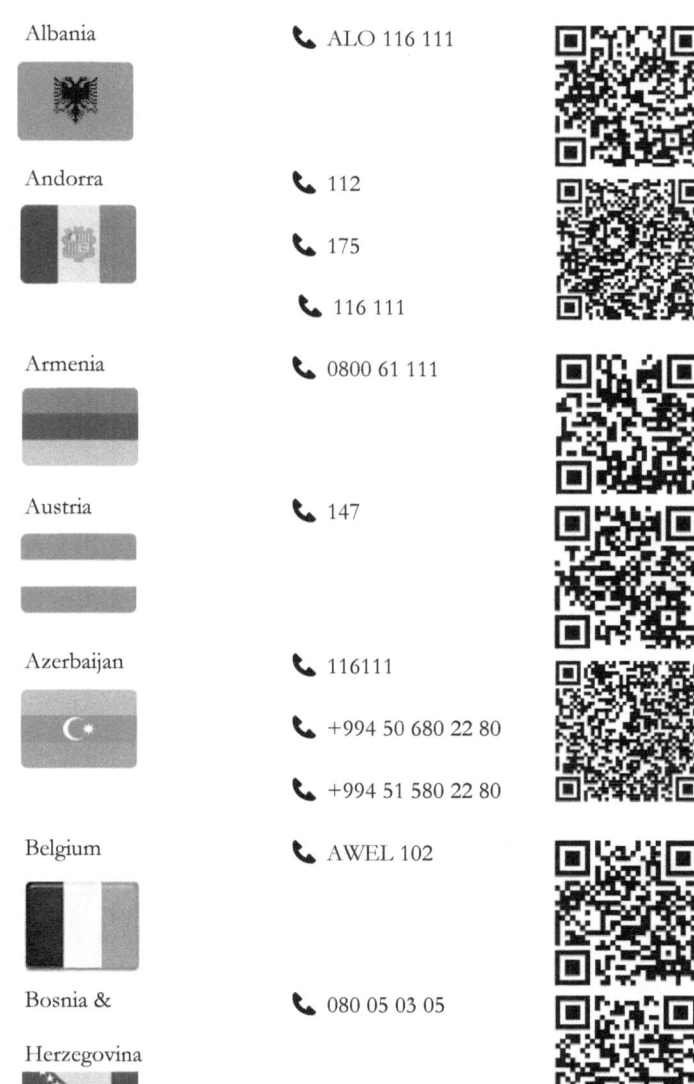

Country	Number
Albania	ALO 116 111
Andorra	112
	175
	116 111
Armenia	0800 61 111
Austria	147
Azerbaijan	116111
	+994 50 680 22 80
	+994 51 580 22 80
Belgium	AWEL 102
Bosnia & Herzegovina	080 05 03 05

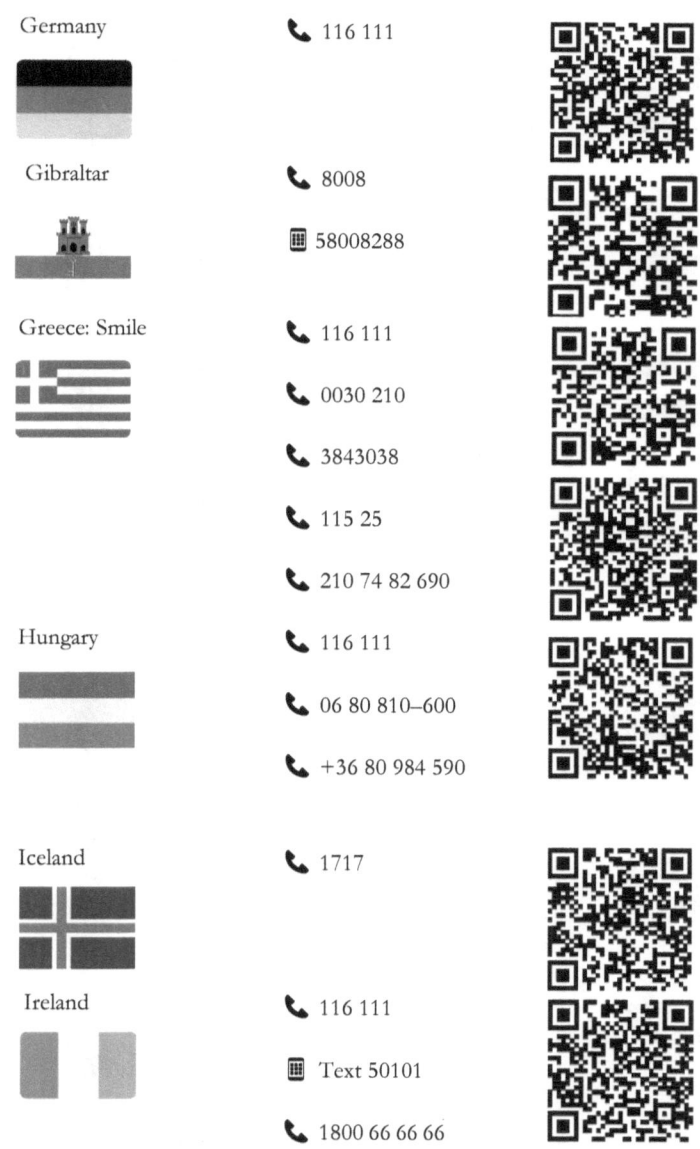

Germany
📞 116 111

Gibraltar
📞 8008
🔢 58008288

Greece: Smile
📞 116 111
📞 0030 210
📞 3843038
📞 115 25
📞 210 74 82 690

Hungary
📞 116 111
📞 06 80 810–600
📞 +36 80 984 590

Iceland
📞 1717

Ireland
📞 116 111
🔢 Text 50101
📞 1800 66 66 66

Country	Phone	
Italy	📞 1 96 96	
Kosovo	📞 0800 12222	
Latvia	📞 116 111 📞 800 6008	
Liechtenstein	📞 147	
Lithuania	📞 116 111	
North Macedonia	📞 +389 70 390 632	
Norway	📞 116 111 📞 800 333 21	

Country	Phone	
Pan EUROPE	112 1177 90101 166 000	
Poland	116 111	
Portugal	116 111	
Romania	116 111	
San Marino	+378 0549 994111 +378 346 725 4983 +378 366 906 7192	
Serbia	116 111	
Slovakia	116 111 0800 500 500	

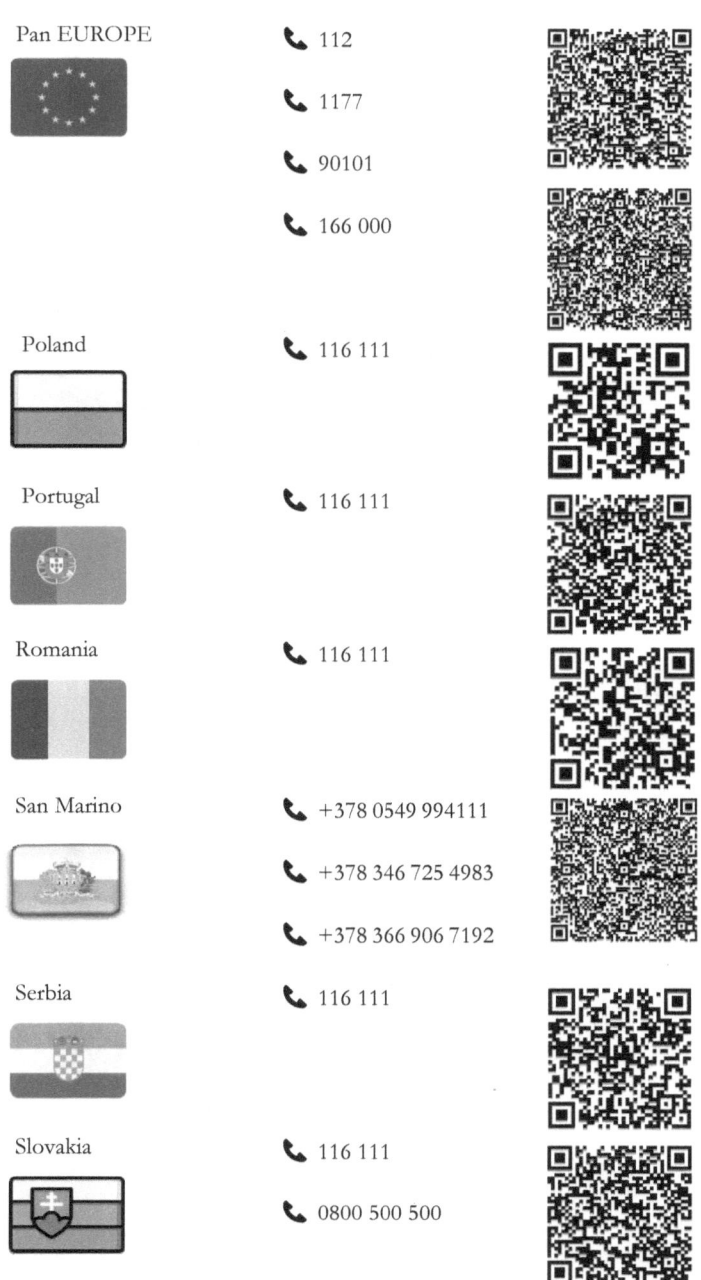

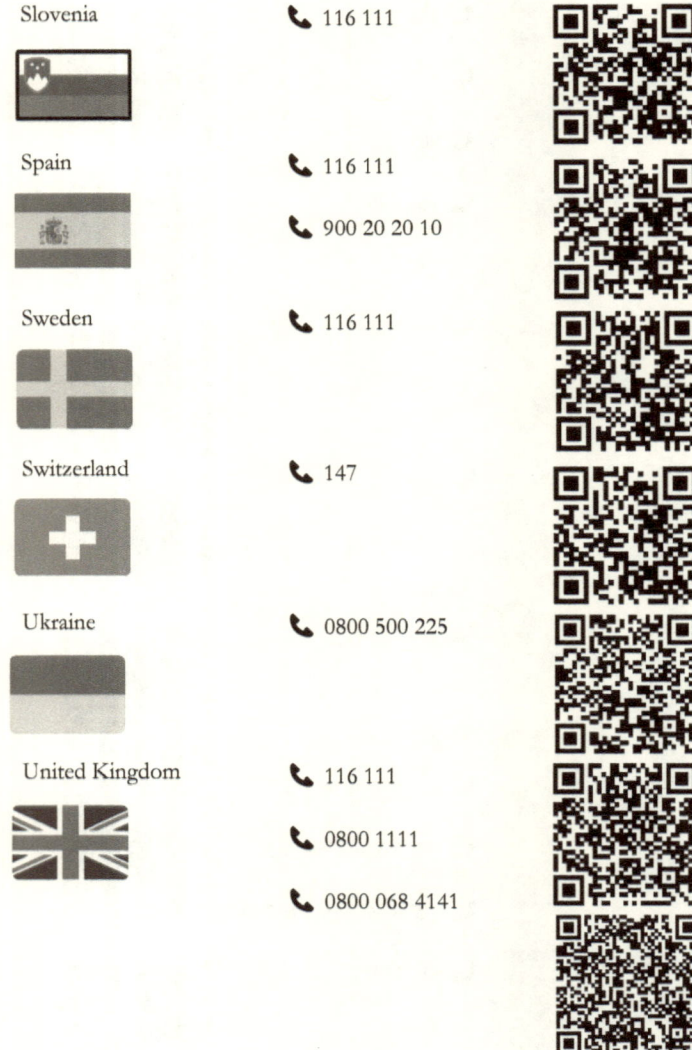

AMERICAS & THE CARIBBEAN

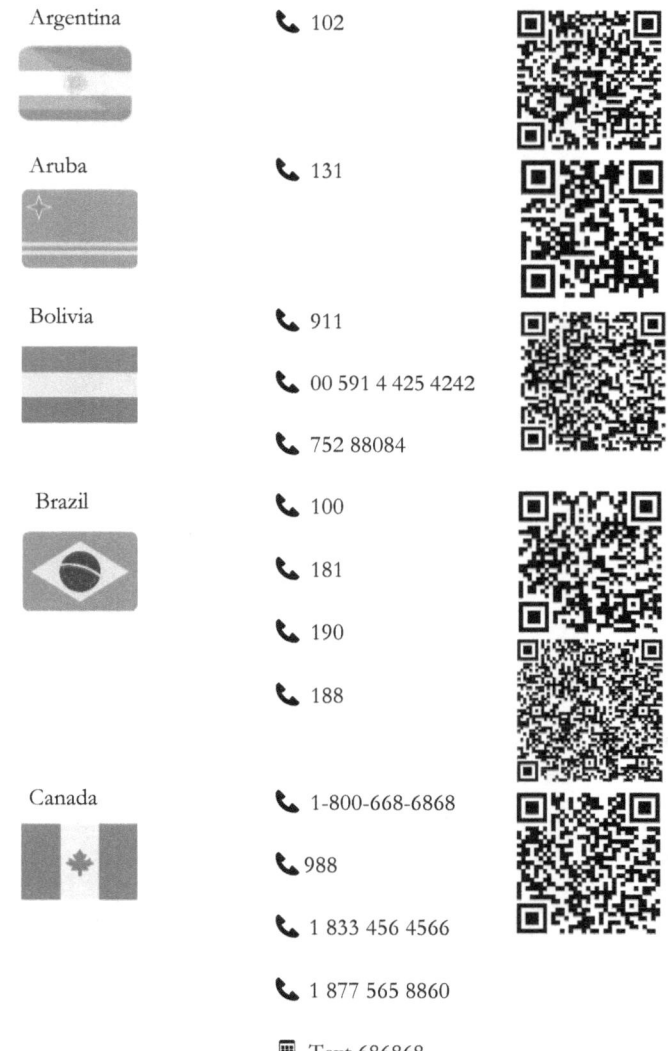

Country	Contact
Argentina	📞 102
Aruba	📞 131
Bolivia	📞 911 📞 00 591 4 425 4242 📞 752 88084
Brazil	📞 100 📞 181 📞 190 📞 188
Canada	📞 1-800-668-6868 📞 988 📞 1 833 456 4566 📞 1 877 565 8860 📱 Text 686868

Country	Phone	QR
Chile - Fonoinfancia	800 200818 1515	
Colombia - ICBF	141 106	
Costa Rica	1147	
Curaçao	918	
Dominican Republic	809 636 3507	
Jamaica	888-SAFE-SPOT	
Ecuador	911 +1 305 509 1176	

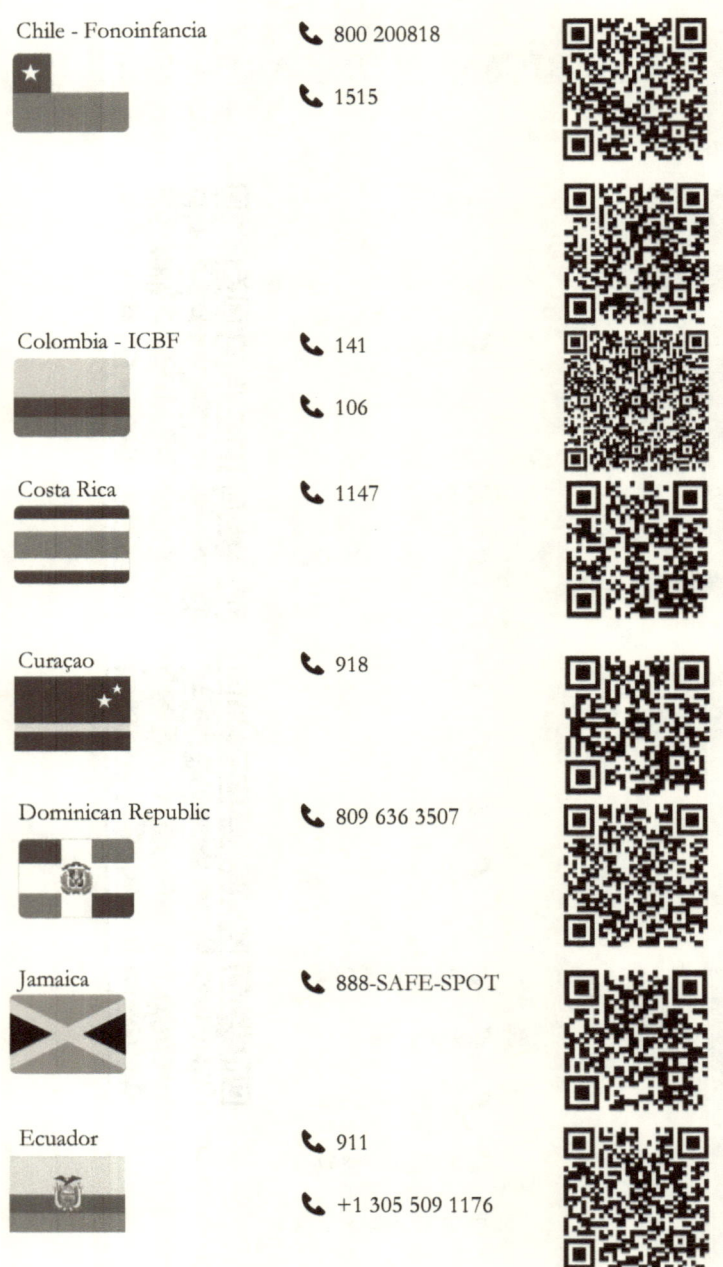

Country	Phone Numbers	
Guyana	914 (592) 264-2293 (592) 223-3500/2	
Mexico	988 (55) 5259-8121 (55) 5804-644 5804-4879 (55) 5655-3080 800-953-1704	
Paraguay	147 133	
Peru	(01) 273-8026 (01) 498-2711	
Suriname - KJT Mi Lijn	123 +597-123 +597-850-6907	

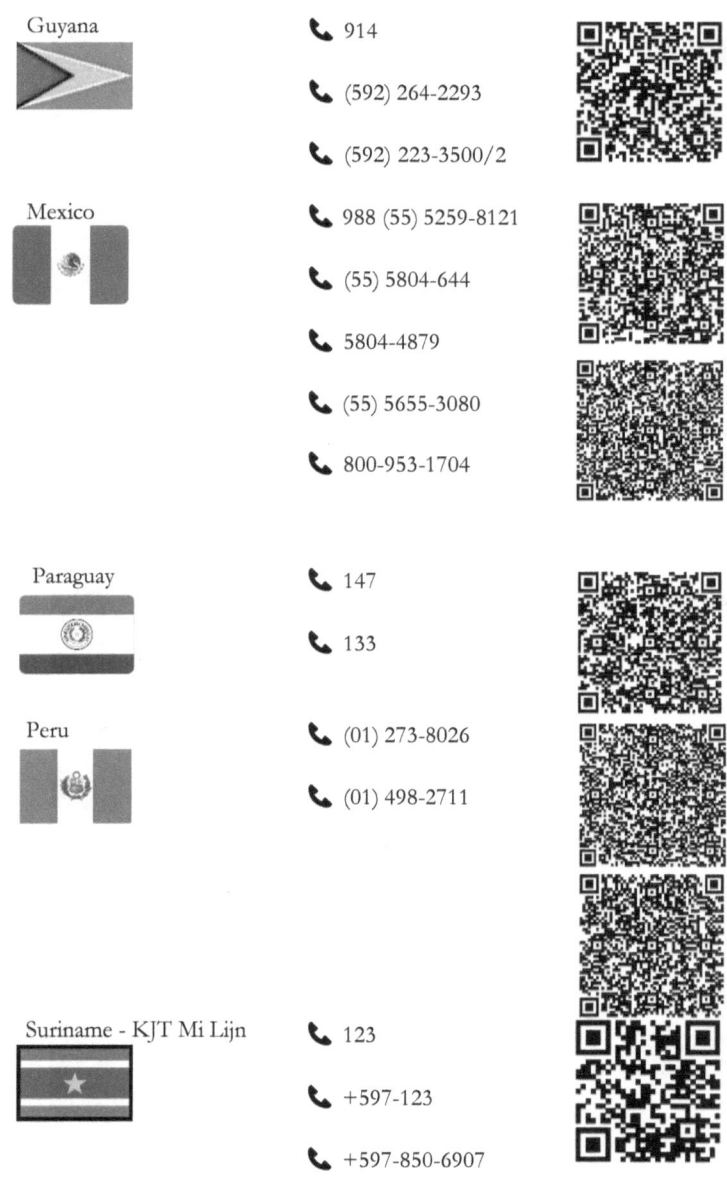

Trinidad & Tobago	📞 131 📞 800-4321	
Uruguay	📞 0800 5050 📞 2915 📞 7317 - 2915 0712	
USA Youth Helpline	📞 888-222-2228 📞 839863 📞 877-968-8491	
Boys Town National Hotline	📞 1-800-448-3000	
Crisis Text Line	📱 TEXT 741741	
USA: National Hotline	📞 1-800-4-A-CHILD 📞 1-800-422-4453	
USA: Polaris	📞 1-888-373-7888 📞 TTY:711 📱 Text BeFree 233733	
USA: Stop It Now!	📞 1.888.PREVENT	

USA: The Trevor Project	866-488-7386	
	TextSTART678678	
Venezuela	911	

MIDDIE EAST & NORTH AFRICA

Country	Phone
Algeria	3033
Bahrain	998
	80008001
Egypt	16000
	021 88531109
Iraq	116
Jordan	110
Kuwait	147
Lebanon Higher Council	01 381 436
	01 388 107
	03 357 695

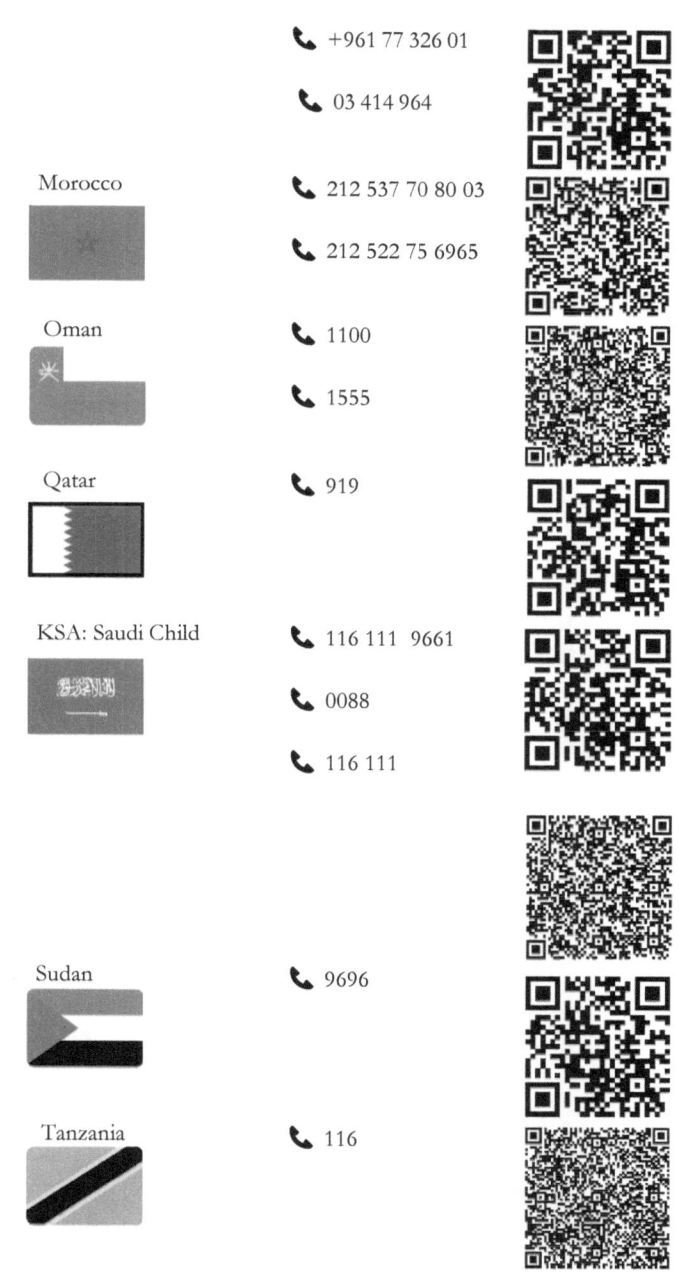

Country	Phone
Morocco	+961 77 326 01 / 03 414 964 / 212 537 70 80 03 / 212 522 75 6965
Oman	1100 / 1555
Qatar	919
KSA: Saudi Child	116 111 9661 / 0088 / 116 111
Sudan	9696
Tanzania	116

Tunisia

- 1809
- 1899

UAE

- 116111
- 800 700
- 800988
- 8002626
- 800 111
- SMS to 8002828
- 800HOP

Yemen

- +967 736 660 660

AFRICA

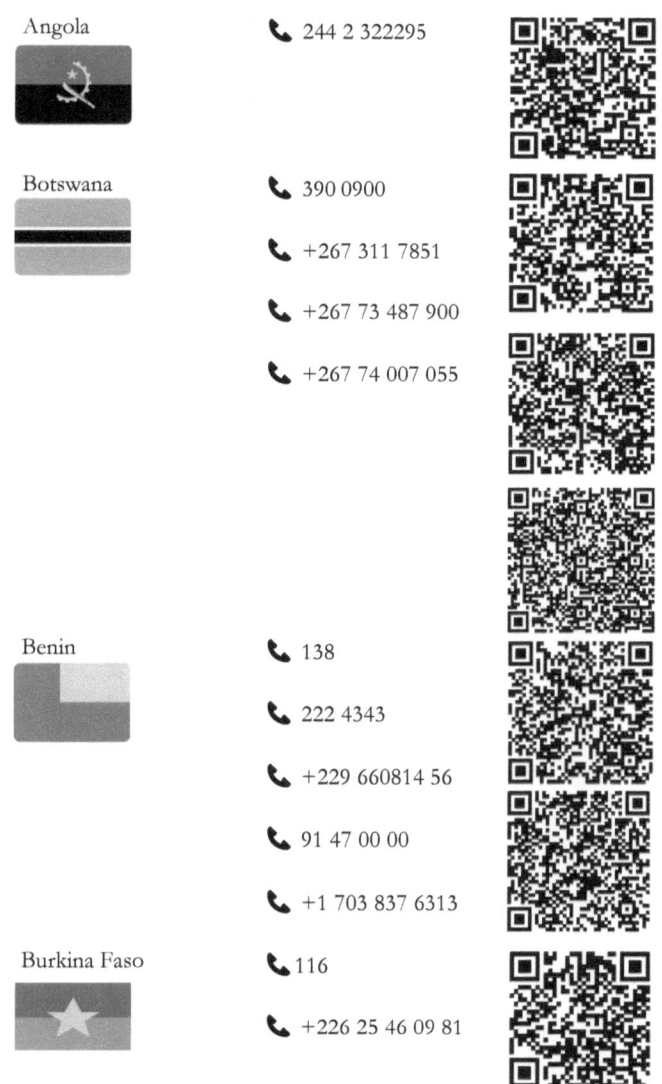

Angola
- 244 2 322295

Botswana
- 390 0900
- +267 311 7851
- +267 73 487 900
- +267 74 007 055

Benin
- 138
- 222 4343
- +229 660814 56
- 91 47 00 00
- +1 703 837 6313

Burkina Faso
- 116
- +226 25 46 09 81

Country	Phone
Burundi	📞 116
Cameroon	📞 116 📞 222 23 25 50
Cape Verde	📞 132 📞 800 2008 📞 23820605500
CA Republic	📞 +236 75 74 09 38 📞 1212
Chad	📞 Police 17/18
Comoros	📞 Police 17/18
Congo	📞 117 📞 00243 815 813 945
Côte d'Ivoire	📞 116

Djibouti	📞 1525 📞 Police 17/18	
Equatorial Guinea	📞 Police 113/114	
Eritrea	📞 Police 113/114	
Eswatini	📞 116 📞 9664 📞 951	
Ethiopia	📞 919 📞 00251221 📞 117575	
Gabon	📞 116 📞 1412	

Country	Phone	
Gambia	116	
Ghana	055 100 0900 0800 900 900	
Guinea	116 +224 621 75 35 35	
Kenya	116	
Lesotho	116 8002 2345	
Liberia	+231777521443 +231886521443	
Libya	091 712 7644 091 002 7717 092 276 7166	

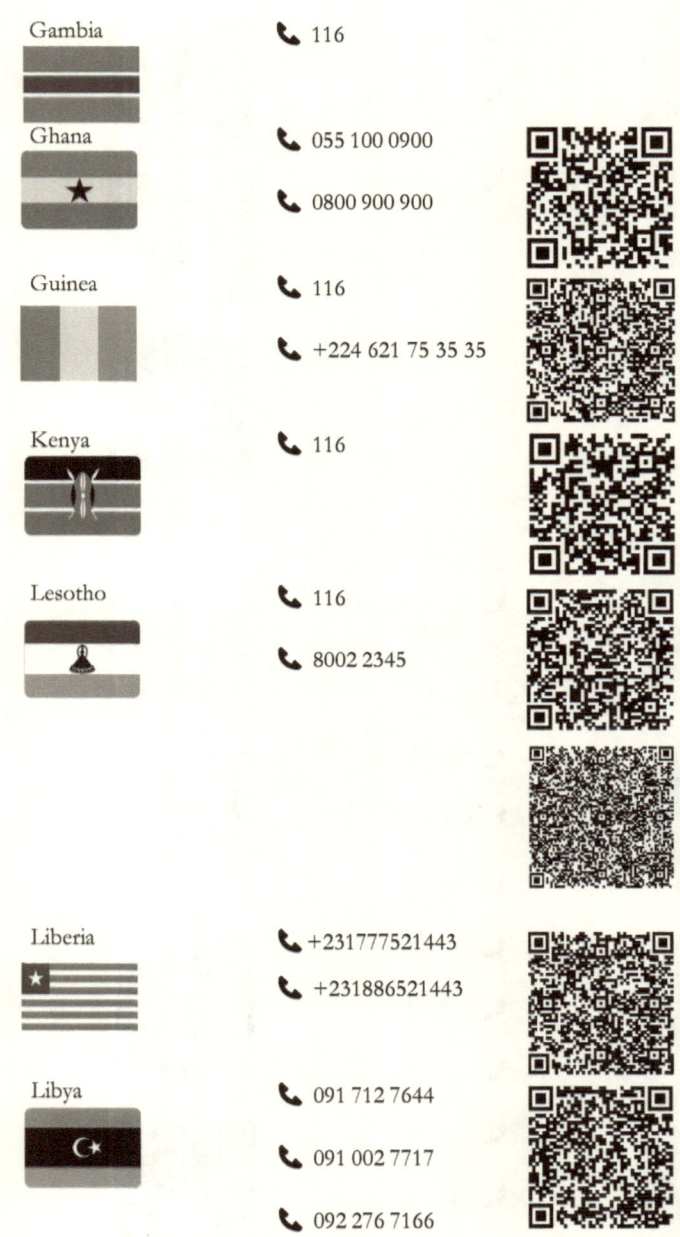

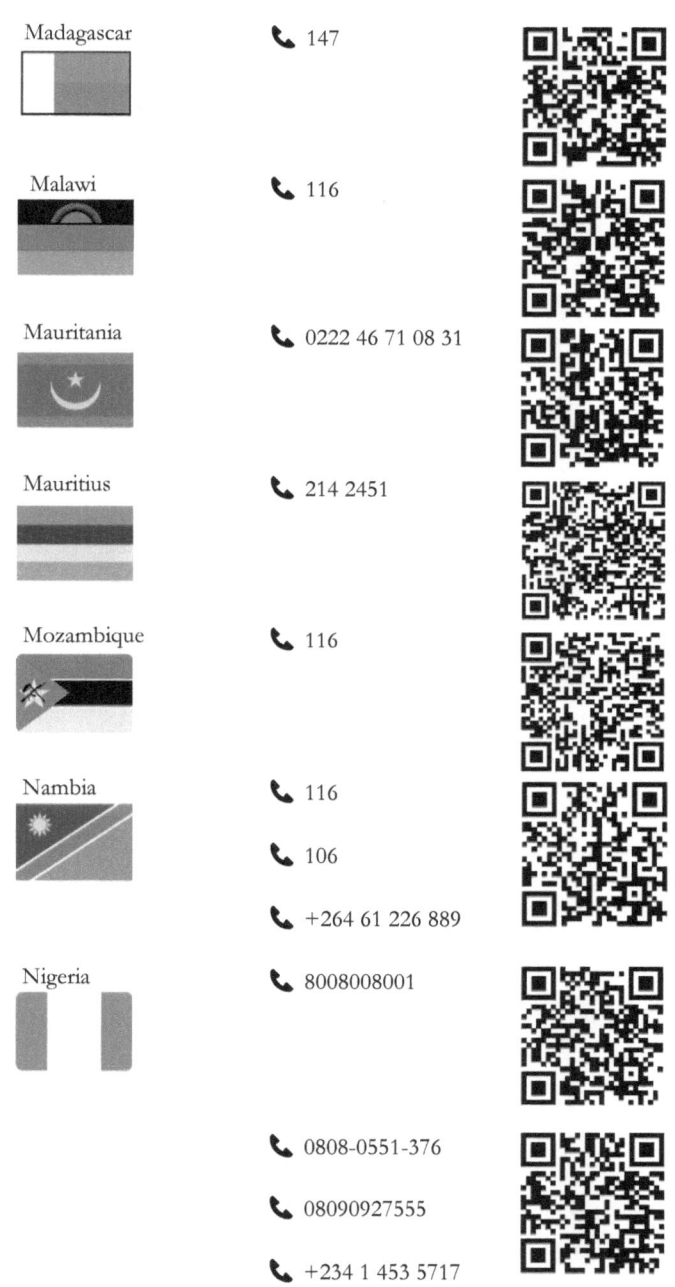

Country	Phone
Madagascar	147
Malawi	116
Mauritania	0222 46 71 08 31
Mauritius	214 2451
Mozambique	116
Nambia	116 / 106 / +264 61 226 889
Nigeria	8008008001 / 0808-0551-376 / 08090927555 / +234 1 453 5717

Country	Numbers
Rwanda	116; 3512
São Tomé & Príncipe	112; 13 222 22 22
Senegal	116
Seychelles	116; 151
Sierra Leone	116; 19; +232 22 000112
Somalia	116; +252 61 333 3166
Somaliland	334
South Africa	116

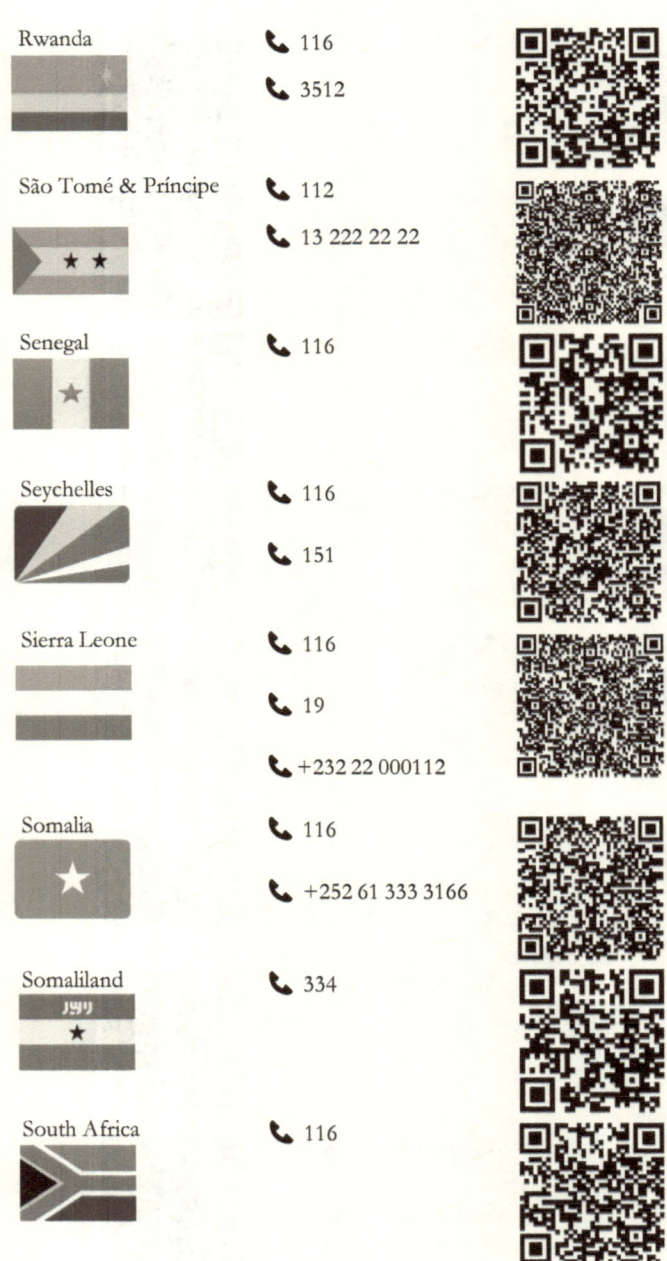

Country	Numbers
South Sudan	9696, 116
Tanzania	116
Togo	1011
Tunisia	1899, 1809
Uganda	116
Western Sahara	116, 150
Zambia	116

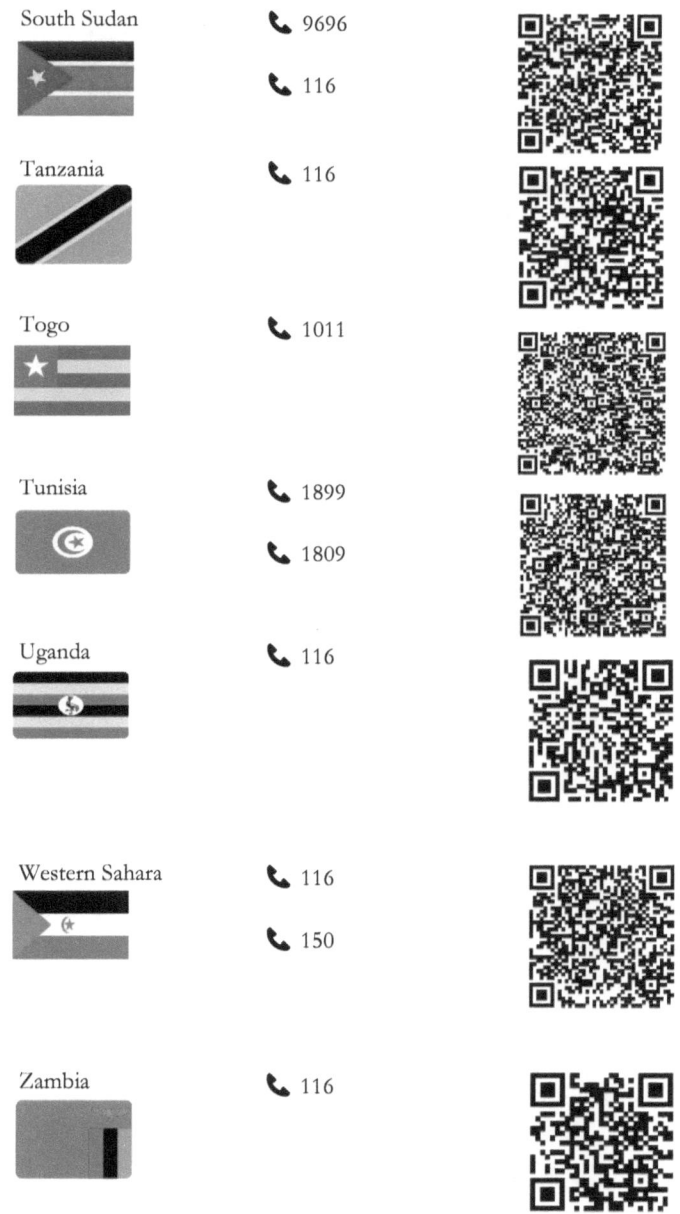

Zimbabwe   📞 116

ASIA & PACIFIC

Australia
📞 1 800 55 1800

Lifeline Australia
📞 13 11 14

Bravehearts
📞 1800 272 831

1800RESPECT
📞 1800 737 732

Bangladesh
📞 1098

Brunei
📞 121

Bhutan
📞 1098

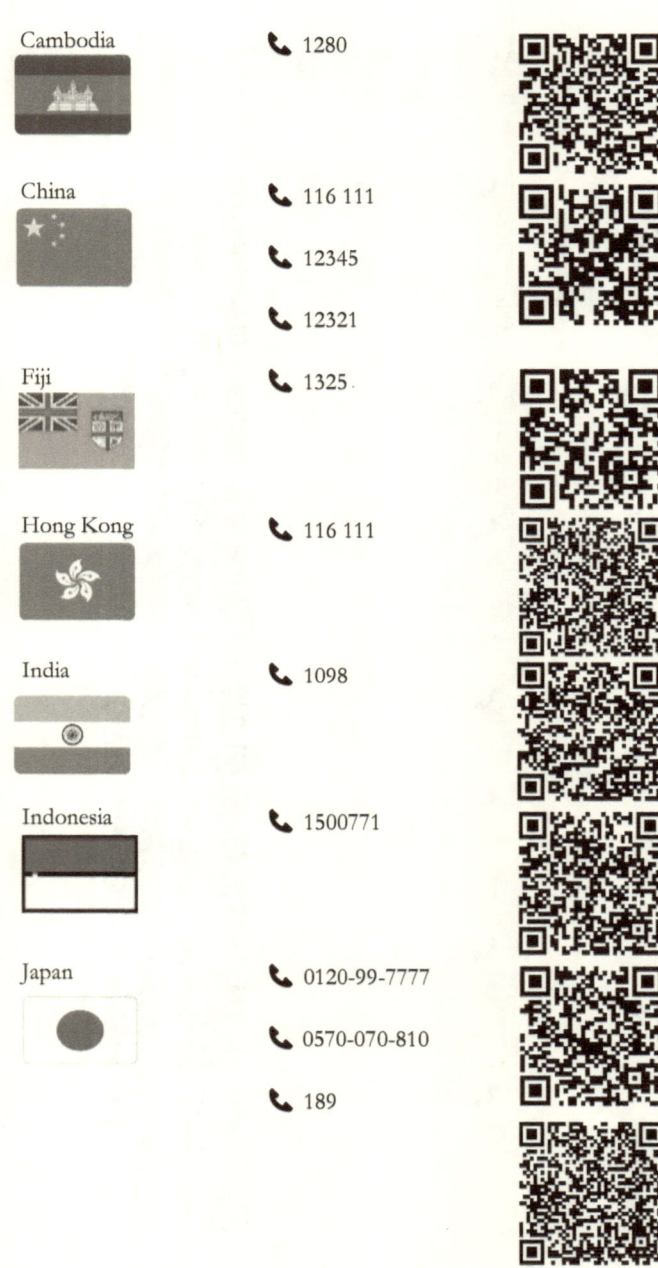

Cambodia	📞 1280
China	📞 116 111
	📞 12345
	📞 12321
Fiji	📞 1325
Hong Kong	📞 116 111
India	📞 1098
Indonesia	📞 1500771
Japan	📞 0120-99-7777
	📞 0570-070-810
	📞 189

Kazakhstan	📞 150	
Korea	📞 1388	
	📞 1398	
	📞 1577-5432	
	📞 02-338-5801~2	
	📞 (800) 854-7771	
	📞 998	
	📞 1588-9191	
Counsel24	📞 1566-2525	
Mental Health Center Crisis Counseling	Seoul Hotline: 📞 (2) 715 8600 📞 (2) 716 8600 📞 (2) 717 8600 📞 (2) 718 8600 Cheju Hotline:	

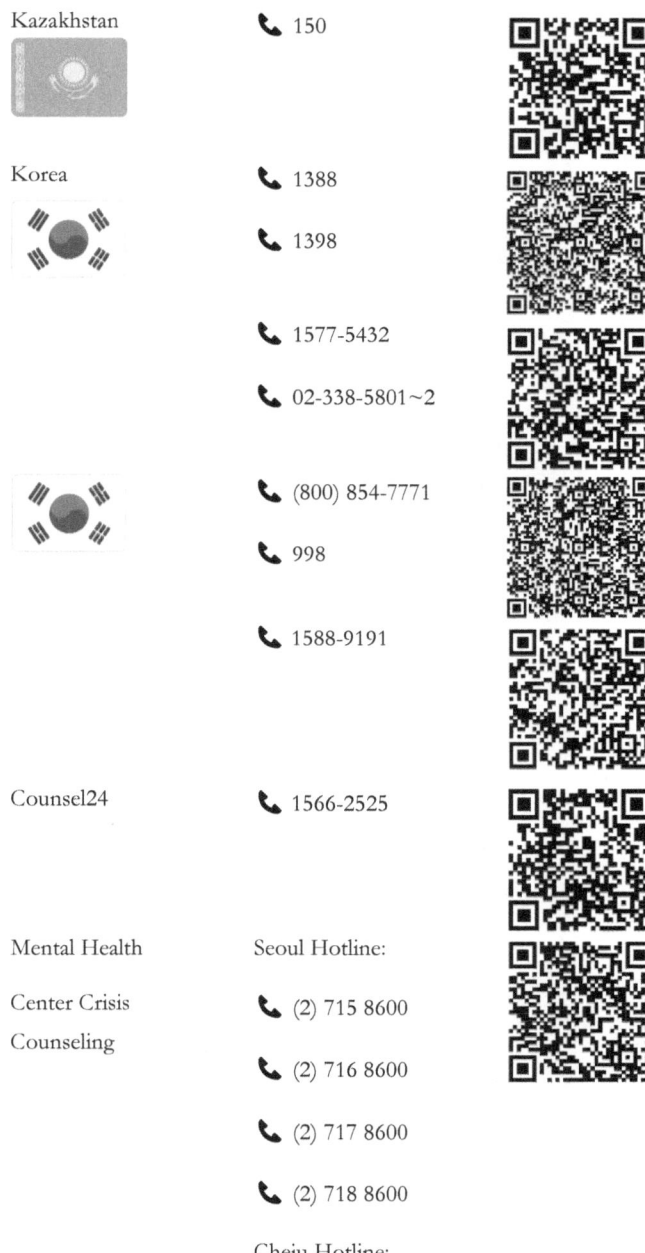

299

📞 (064) 52 9191

Choongju Hotline:

📞 (0441) 847-9191

Chunju Hotline:

📞 (0652) 86-9191

Inchon Hotline:

📞 (032) 421 9191

Puchon Hotline:

📞 (032) 663-9191

Pohang Hotline:

📞 (0562) 72-9191

📞 (0525) 21-9191

Ulsan Hotline:

📞 (0522) 67-9191

Pusan Hotline:

📞 (051) 807-9191

Kyrgyzstan

📞 111

📞 123

Laos	📞 192	
Maldives	📞 1412	
Mongolia	📞 108	
Nepal	📞 1098	
New Zealand	📞 +64 800 942 8787 📞 0800 376633 📱 Text 234	

Lifeline Aotearoa	📞 0800 543 354	
Samaritans Aotearoa	📞 0800 726 666	
Need to Talk?	📞 1737	
	📞 0800 611 116	
	📞 0800 933 922	
Pakistan	📞 1098	
Papua New Guinea	📞 +675 7150 8000	
Philippines	📞 163	

Country	Hotline	QR
Singapore	📞 1800 2744 788	
Sri Lanka	📞 1929	
Taiwan	📞 113 📞 +886 2 8195 3005	
Citizen Hotline (Taipei)	📞 1999 📞 02-2720-8889 📞 +886-2-8195-3005	
Tajikistan	📞 +992 44 600 0190	
Thailand	📞 1387	
Vanuatu	📞 87777	
Vietnam	📞 111	

www.ingramcontent.com/pod-product-compliance
Lightning Source LLC
Chambersburg PA
CBHW020356080526
44584CB00014B/1050